Will She Be

Will She Be Right?

The Future of Australia

Herman Kahn
and
Thomas Pepper

University of Queensland Press

© University of Queensland Press, St Lucia, Queensland, 1980

Typeset by Press Etching Pty Ltd, Brisbane
Printed and bound by Watson Ferguson & Co., Brisbane

Distributed in the United Kingdom, Europe, the Middle East, Africa, and the Caribbean by Prentice-Hall International, International Book Distributors Ltd, 66 Wood Lane End, Hemel Hempstead, Herts., England.

National Library of Australia
Cataloguing-in-Publication data

Kahn, Herman, 1922-
    Will She Be Right?

    Index.
    Bibliography.
    ISBN 0 7022 1568 6.
    ISBN 0 7022 1569 4 Paperback.

    1. Australia - Economic conditions.
    i. Pepper, Thomas, 1939-, joint author.
    2. Title.

330.994'063

Contents

Tables

Figures

Acknowledgments

This study was undertaken as a joint project of Hudson Institute
and P.G. Pak-Poy & Associates Pty Ltd, and was supported by
grants from fourteen Australian corporations:
Australia and New Zealand Banking Group Limited
Australian Consolidated Industries Limited
A.W. Baulderstone Pty Limited
BT Australia Limited
Bank of New South Wales
The Broken Hill Proprietery Company Limited
Consolidated Gold Fields Australia Limited
Conzinc Riotinto of Australia Limited
IBM Australia Limited
Jennings Industries Limited
M.I.M. Holdings Limited
The Myer Emporium Limited
The Shell Company of Australia Limited
Utah Development Company
We are extremely grateful to the sponsoring companies, not
only for their financial support, but also for their general support
of the concept that a study of Australia in a long-term and world-
wide context would be a useful contribution to Australian society.
We are particularly grateful to V.E. Jennings, Executive Director-
Research, of Jennings Industries, and to Sir Roderick Carnegie,
Chairman and Chief Executive of Conzinc Riotinto of Australia,
for their encouragement and assistance in helping to launch the
study, as well as their continued intellectual and moral support
throughout the project.

We are also grateful to numerous people in these various companies who took time to assist us in many ways, including sharing their views and providing useful material. In particular, we are grateful to James Byth, Advisor, Public Policy, Kenneth D. Gott of the International Relations staff, and John D.S. Macleod, Chief Economist, all of C.R.A., who made available a considerable amount of published and bibliographical material and who spoke to us at length about matters within their respective fields; John Brunner, Chief Economist, and Peter Duminy, of the Public Affairs staff, at B.H.P., who were similarly generous with useful material and with their own views; Jillian R. Broadbent, Associate Director and Corporate Economist, BT Australia, who prepared a background paper on the structure of the capital market; and Alvin A. Hirsch, former Managing Director of BT Australia, who prepared a memorandum comparing Australian financial policies with those of other economies in the Asia-Pacific region.

Throughout the country, we were received with warmth and encouragement. On two of our visits, we were privileged to have met with Prime Minister Fraser and members of his staff, as well as with representatives of various federal departments. We were fortunate also to have had a series of meetings with state government officials in Brisbane, Sydney, Melbourne, Adelaide, and Perth. In particular, Sir Charles Court, Premier of Western Australia and a friend for many years, and the Honourable Andrew Mensaros, Minister for Works, Water Resources, and Minister Assisting the Minister Coordinating Economic and Regional Development and Housing, spent considerable time giving us their views. Many other individuals from various walks of life kindly shared their ideas on the future of Australia. We are grateful to all for their time and hospitality.

Several people were of great help in discussing certain points in detail and in reading and commenting on portions of the manuscript. In this regard, we wish to thank Dr Ashton Calvert; S.J. Janow; Ambassador John Menadue; Dr John Paterson; Richard W. Rabinowitz; Takeshi Sakurauchi; and Dr Kyoko Sheridan.

The book draws on material prepared for the final report of the first stage of the study, prepared by Justin Brenan, Peter H.

Edmonds, David Hain, Patrick G. Pak-Poy, and John Paterson of P.G. Pak-Poy & Associates, and Rudy L. Ruggles Jr, former president of Hudson and a major contributor to earlier phases of the project, Douglas A. Cayne, John B. Trammell, and the undersigned of Hudson Institute.

Several members of the Hudson staff made major contributions to the final manuscript. In particular, John B. Trammell and Alan Woodhull, consultants to the Institute, worked tirelessly to assist us in research and in revising and rewriting preliminary drafts. Studies by Irving Leveson and Jane Newitt were of great value in the preparation of Chapters 4 and 5. Jimmy W. Wheeler assisted in the preparation of material on Industrial structure shifts and made many valuable comments on various drafts. Ernest Schneider provided invaluable editorial assistance, and helped us to clarify and sharpen many ideas.

We also want to thank the many typists and assistants who helped put the manuscript together, often at great inconvenience to their schedules, and who prepared many of the accompanying charts: Dorothy Worfolk, Roberta McPheeters, Judith Jacono, Maureen Pritchard, Maud Bonnell, Mary Mitchell, and Ceci Floren at the Institute's head office, and Michiko Moribe, Chizuko Harada, Kang Chung-shin, Sarah Loh, Yayoi Ohta, and Kimiko Seki at Hudson's Asia-Pacific office.

Finally, we wish to thank Frank Thompson, manager of the University of Queensland Press, and Merril Yule, head of the editorial department, for making it possible to publish this book, and in particular for their patience and understanding in the face of delays at our end.

The above persons and companies all helped us to complete this book, but we alone are responsible for its contents.

Herman Kahn
Thomas Pepper

April 1980
Croton-on-Hudson, N.Y.
and Tokyo

Introduction

This book outlines what we believe are the major issues facing Australia for the next ten to twenty years and beyond. We have concentrated on economic issues, and to a lesser degree political issues, both domestic and international. We mention various social, cultural, and technological issues, though we do not deal with them in detail. Indeed, the book as a whole is more general than specific, but that, we feel, can be a strength as well as a weakness.

We have looked at Australia in terms of two basic contexts (1) the future of world economic development, and (2) the future of the Asia-Pacific region. More specifically, we have sought to analyze Australia's economic prospects as one of six-teen advanced capitalist nations (ACNs) in a world in which the middle-income countries will be playing an increasing role as engines of growth.[1] We see world economic development as a process of moving from a pre-industrial to industrial and super-industrial stages, and eventually to a post-industrial stage, and we see contemporary Australia as being in the forefront of this pro-cess — in some ways too much so. Our analysis and policy recom-mendations, to the degree that we make recommendations, centre on how Australia might either cope with or influence this process.

We also believe that much of the spur that the middle-income countries will give to world economic growth will occur in, and stem from, the growth of countries in the Asia-Pacific region. By Asia-Pacific region, we refer to a hybrid group of countries that generally border on the Pacific, but that are linked to one another less by their physical location or historical ties than by a common orientation to economic growth (relative to other countries of comparable GNP per capita) and by an increasing degree of interdependence. Thus, we include in this region not only Japan and China and the other high-growth countries of East and Southeast Asia and the United States, Canada, Australia, and New Zealand (all of which have increasing ties with East and Southeast Asia), but also the high-growth countries of Latin America, such as Brazil and Mexico, which also have increasing ties with other Asia-Pacific countries. In other words, the Asia-Pacific region is defined by its economic, rather than its physical, geography. Australia, along with the United States, Canada, and New Zealand, belongs to the Asia-Pacific region, though all four countries can also be regarded as having an Atlantic-Protestant culture.[2]

We have tried to relate events in Australia to trends in world economic development and the Asia-Pacific region and vice versa. Although Australia is more affected by world trends than the rest of the world is affected by trends in Australia, we believe Australia is ahead of other countries in some aspects of the progression from pre-industrial to post-industrial society. Thus, we think it is useful for the rest of the world to understand more of what is going on in Australia.

This study was first conceived as an outgrowth of the authors' participation in a Pacific Institute seminar in Melbourne in February 1977. We met at that time with representatives of six major Australian corporations, and discussed the idea of a study of the future of Australia in a long-term and world-wide context. With the support of eleven corporations (joined later by three more), we began formal work on the project in early 1978.

In any country study such as this, both the perspective of an outsider and that of an insider have corresponding strengths and weaknesses. Perhaps understandably, we have concentrated on what we feel are the strengths of an outsider's perspective. We have tried to outline a range of alternative futures for Australia in as detached a manner as possible. With the Australian bicentennial coming up in 1988, this is a natural time to review the past and look ahead to the future. We hope this study will stimulate considerable discussion of the directions and goals of Australian society, and at the same time contribute to a greater understanding of Australia elsewhere in the world.

Notes

1. This and other terminology in the introduction are discussed in detail in Chapter 2. The other nations in the ACN category, as used here, are: the United States, the United Kingdom, the Federal Republic of Germany, France, Italy, Canada, Japan, the Netherlands, Belgium, Denmark, Norway, Sweden, Finland, Switzerland, and Austria.
2. The other countries with an Atlantic-Protestant culture are: the United Kingdom, the Netherlands, Denmark, Sweden, and Norway. The term Atlantic-Protestant does not mean that everyone in the society is either "Atlantic" or Protestant, only that the dominant mores of these countries are similar enough to warrant their being grouped together in a way that emphasizes the bourgeois capitalism and religious tolerance found in these countries for most of the past 200 years. Many of the Atlantic-Protestant countries, notably the U.S., Canada, Australia, and the Netherlands, have large Roman Catholic populations, but the dominant mores of these countries (and to some extent even of the Catholic churches themselves) are still more "Protestant" than Catholic (e.g., emphasizing a separation of church and state, and the individual's right to question authority). These characteristics are less strongly felt in countries with a predominantly Catholic culture; or in the neo-Confucian countries of East and Southeast Asia. It is perhaps more than a coincidence that the Atlantic-Protestant countries (plus Switzerland, which is significantly Protestant) are almost the only countries where liberal democracy has taken root, uninterruptedly, for more than two to three generations.

ONE

Alternative Futures for Australia

Is the future of Australia — this vast, isolated country — a possible model of what lies ahead for the rest of the world? If the archetypal bumper sticker on a Sydney vehicle says unabashedly, "I'd rather be sailing", might not the rest of us drop what we are doing and go sailing ourselves? This question, so seemingly Australian, will probably become just as relevant to other developed countries. Once sailing — or recreation generally — is accepted as an alternative to work, the decision remains of how much time to spend on leisure and how much on work. The crucial issue is one of trade-offs.

In looking at Australia today, and at a range of possible future Australias, it has been useful to assume that this country might well be a prototype for the rest of the world. In particular, four possible futures seem most likely and relevant for Australia. These involve, respectively, an emphasis on:

1. A "business-as-usual" society, an Australia that continues more or less along current lines.
2. An early emergence of an Australian-style, welfare- and leisure-oriented, more or less post-industrial society.
3. A "reformed" or sensibly protectionist Australia, in which the protectionism is more selective and more efficient than at present.
4. An Australia with a distinctly more dynamic economy, achieved mainly through a greatly increased emphasis on free market forces, and probably an increased rate of immigration as well.

Australia is, of course, an atypical country. Paradoxically, this makes it especially interesting. As a relatively isolated area, Australia can follow certain trends in a pure and unobstructed way, which could hardly happen in an area that interacted more intimately with the rest of the world. Canada, for example, is so close to the United States, culturally as well as geographically, that it cannot afford to fall too far behind the U.S. in per capita income, lest this lead to resentment and political unrest. Similarly, the countries of western Europe have a generally symbiotic relationship with one another, though this is felt less deeply by Great Britain and Ireland than by their continental neighbours; such a long-held tradition of isolation would typically take more than a generation to change. Australia is part of the Atlantic-Protestant cultural area, and its isolation has allowed it to retain many traditional aspects of this culture, even while introducing many innovations. Moreover, an extraordinary endowment of land and natural resources gives Australia a degree of freedom that helps to protect the country from some of the disadvantages of isolation. Thus, Australians can take certain possibilities seriously that would not be feasible elsewhere. Even so, the issue is still one of degree: granted that a resource-rich, relatively developed, relatively isolated Australia has many reasons to consider itself "the lucky country", Australians must always ask themselves whether their luck will run out if they continue to follow current policies.

The four alternatives listed above represent a realistic range of choices open to Australia for the next ten to twenty years. None of the four represents a sharp break with current trends; indeed, two of them might even be described as variations on a business-as-usual Australia. This relatively circumscribed range of choices does not apply beyond the next two decades, but the course followed during this interval may make a great deal of difference to the kind of Australia that emerges in the twenty-first century, and to the kinds of choices and challenges the country is likely to face at that time. Until then, it is hard to envisage a plausible "disaster" scenario specifically applicable to Australia — such as a direct external military threat or an endless series of internal conflicts — no matter which of these paths is taken. To be sure, the future is always unknowable, and Australia might get into serious trouble, but this prospect is not as likely in the next ten to twenty years as one of the four alternatives mentioned. This estimate is discussed in detail in the concluding chapter. This chapter outlines the four most likely alternative futures, as well as a range of less likely possibilities considered for purposes of contrast. Of course, any big change in the external world would be reflected in Australia and at the present moment it is not too difficult to write disaster scenarios based on uncontrollable inflation, some intense crisis in the Persian Gulf, or even U.S./Soviet military conflict. But in this study we ignore these sudden and difficult-to-predict disasters in the external world and concentrate on alternatives for Australia within a generally familiar external environment.

A Business-as-Usual Australia

A business-as-usual Australia would continue to be relatively empty, rich, urban, sports-loving, and unionized, as well as predominantly Caucasian; it would also be increasingly inefficient, uncompetitive, and isolated, except in certain sectors of the economy with strong links to other countries or to multinational companies or other transnational phenomena. In contemplating this picture, most Australians might well feel happily isolated from the economic, social, political, and technological changes going on elsewhere, and, on balance, quite pleased to live in what seems perhaps the most comfortable, agreeable place on earth in this latter part of the twentieth century. However, one question arises: will a business-as-usual alternative enable Australia to remain as comfortable and agreeable — compared with other developed countries — when it enters the twenty-first century a scant two decades from now?

An Australian who looks at the country's record of economic development, and then looks ahead to the end of the century, might be either comforted or disturbed: comforted because growth rates remain high enough to maintain the affluence that already exists, or worried because recent growth rates are lower than those of many other countries. Both conclusions could be drawn from the data.

A business-as-usual Australia is the most likely of the four alternatives: a continuation of current economic trends, both internal and external, with more of the stagflation now plaguing virtually all developed countries. Indeed, although these countries face an extended period of economic and social malaise, Australia's recovery from the worst effects of the 1972-74 commodity price increases and the subsequent world recession has been even less dynamic than others. This suggests that, in the absence of concerted efforts, it may be extremely difficult for Australia to outperform other developed nations during the 1980s.

Many trends in Australian psychology and social structure reinforce the economic pressures for a business-as-usual alternative. The well-known phrase incorporated into the title of this book, "she'll be right", is more than a mere assertion of naivete. The notion that things will go right is so deeply felt by "dinky-di Aussies" that it is doubtless a product of Australian history. This "no worries" attitude is more than fatalism, or a reliance on God's will: rather it is a feeling that one can afford to ignore the consequences of one's actions because things have worked out in the past, and probably will in the future. By and large, things have "gone right", even though Australia's current relative prosperity can be interpreted as either comforting or disturbing, as suggested earlier.

Still, obstacles have been overcome. Australia did achieve a relatively high degree of economic development in a remarkably short time; between 1860 and 1890, it was the richest country in the world on a per capita basis. Against seemingly massive odds, the continent was tamed, at least the more habitable areas where settlers chose to live. Australia's war record is admirable. The successful assimilation of a whole new wave of ethnic groups in the postwar period is further evidence that Australians can make things go "right". In other words, however easy-going Australians may appear to be (and claim to be), they do get things done. The place works — most of the time.

Moreover, Australia has been lucky. Its early European settlers succeeded in establishing a viable society. Strong feelings of sectionalism have never erupted into civil war, or reached the kind of divisiveness now plaguing Canada, Spain, or even the U.K. The distance between Australia and Britain was indeed great, and fears of the rising power of Germany at the end of the nineteenth century were a major reason for federation. But the British fleet was powerful enough, in fact or reputation, to shield the Australian continent from any serious external military threat for 150 years. When the Japanese threat materialized — the bombing of Darwin in February 1942 was probably the greatest single shock ever to hit Australia — it was quickly counterbalanced by the American alliance. After the defeat of Japan, and as Australians gradually became willing to see postwar Japan as a potential partner rather than a threat, Lang Hancock and others made the lucky mineral finds which lead to the mining boom, and a new era of prosperity commenced.

A business-as-usual approach is also reinforced by the typically Australian concept of "mateship and egalitarianism", which stems in part from the comradeship of men once cast together in the harsh environment of a sheep run or gold mine. It also probably reflects Australia's convict heritage, the loyalty that members of a prison-gang feel for each other, the artificially imposed but still genuine solidarity of people who share an enforced common fate. People in such circumstances often feel a moral imperative to share and share alike.

Indeed, the idea of mateship and egalitarianism is so entrenched that it transcends working-class or lower middle-class categories. Within almost all groups in Australian society, a feeling of camaraderie is probably stronger than in any other country in the Atlantic-Protestant cultural area. Even upper class Australians share the feeling among themselves. The wool growing gentry and their descendants may well feel socially superior to other groups in Australian society, but they generally try to avoid displaying this feeling; they are just as quick as other Australians to criticize people who do stand out too much. This is part of the "knocker" syndrome so often decried by critics who yearn for a sense of mission for Australia. Even genuinely outstanding figures tend to an almost automatic affectation of modesty, lest they be too obviously identified as outstanding, and for that reason subject to "knocking". On the other hand, Australia is

surely the only country where taxi drivers sometimes tip the
customer: for example, if the fare is $1.10, the driver might say,
"Make it a dollar, mate". This is another way of saying, "You're
no better than I am, and I'm no better than you, and among us
mates $1.00 is a nice round number."

Economists disagree as to the effects of differing patterns of
income distribution, particularly the effects of excess income
equality on future growth. Proponents of a higher rate of economic growth generally argue that a certain degree of income inequality promotes a higher rate of growth, and that an emphasis on
equality of current income acts as a disincentive for future
growth. This question lies at the heart of the Conservative-
Labour debate in Britain, for example. In Australia, equality is so
widely celebrated as a social value that the usual terms of the
debate must be modified. Because of this regard for mateship,
proponents of a higher rate of growth for Australia need to show
that, to the extent that economic growth unavoidably creates
some inequality, it need not create "too much", at least in the
minds of native-born Australians. (It would seem that "new
Australians" — or migrants — place a much higher value on
growth, and less on equality, than their "old Australian" com-
patriots, but their views tend to be discounted in typical discussions of this issue.) In general, mateship and egalitarianism make
a business-as-usual alternative more likely than an intensely
dynamic economy particularly since the mateship and egalitarianism do not seem to result in lessened social strife.

Another important Australian attitude is the country's traditional isolationism, which, at least in the current milieu, also
works against a dynamic economy and supports the likelihood of
business-as-usual. This "protect-my-corner" approach is much
broader than an isolationist position with regard to foreign countries. In its basic form, this attitude is much like that of a traditional peasant — not so much hostile to outsiders as simply unin-
volved, and therefore unconcerned: he becomes actively fearful
only when the outside world turns its attention to him. In this
sense, while Australia was as physically separated from the rest of
the world as it was during the nineteenth century, and at the same
time as economically and emotionally linked to Britain, then the

strongest power on earth, its   corner was protected for it. Nine-teenth century Australians evinced this protect-my-corner attitude in a natural and inoffensive, if provincial and narrow-minded, way.

In the different circumstances of the 1980s, a protect-my-cor-ner attitude reflects insecurity and defensiveness vis-à-vis the rest of the world; all too often it can became selfish and even self-destructive. A tolerance for this attitude is one reason for Australia's traditional protection of manufacturing, and the legacy of its once-traditional (and once-inoffensive) White Australia immigration policy. In recent years, this insecure and defensive version of a protect-my-corner stance has led to attempts to assert not only the right to a livelihood, but also the right to a particular kind of livelihood, in a particular place. Whether manifested in opposition to new industries, new tech-nologies, or new Australians, this position is more negative than provincial, and more selfish than courageous. In this form, it is akin to the attitude of low-ranking soldiers or sailors, who often have little or no conception of their overall mission. Their main goals are usually a decent meal, a cold beer, a warm bed, and a girl, and from any viewpoint, except the shortest, these low-level goals are taken too exclusively.

One highly visible manifestation of this version of a protect-my-corner attitude is Australia's habit of lightning strikes, partic-ularly those affecting transportation. Such strikes cause great inconvenience to almost everybody, and are counter-productive by any objective criteria. Certainly the average person would con-clude that 1979's bus strike in Adelaide, when union drivers abandoned passengers in the middle of their routes the day before a state election, did nothing but damage to the union, the trade union movement as a whole, and the state Labor party. Yet such strikes continue to be tolerated, and continue to occur.

Indeed, whereas other developed countries have labour dis-putes and strikes in particular industries or plants, the sort of strikes that are purposely designed to bother the rest of society seem characteristic of Australia.

These attitudes — no worries, mateship and egalitarianism, and protect-my-corner — are more or less natural consequences of Australia's historical experience. In terms of the future, they typify certain characteristics of Australian psychology and social structure that are likely to reinforce economic pressures for a business-as-usual alternative.

However, another widely-held, but less frequently discussed, attitude tends to counter-balance these three: a drive for excellence, a genuine striving for ever-greater achievements. This "striving"   attitude is also part-and-parcel of Australia's past, when it was an obvious prerequisite for accomplishing such tasks as constructing hundreds of miles of fences or digging for ore with pick and shovel. Today, in a relatively affluent but still relatively isolated Australia, a striving attitude is often taken for granted, even though — and partly because — it continues to show up in many different ways. In sport, for example, Australians still want to give the world Olympic-class swimmers like Dawn Fraser and Shane Gould and tennis champions like Ken Rosewall, Rod Laver, and Evonne Goolagong. It took a Nobel Prize to put Patrick White, and by implication all other Australian writers, on the literary map in their own country; but once this self-imposed barrier was crossed, an ever-increasing number of Australian writers, artists, composers, rock stars, and filmmakers have tested themselves against world standards, either by bringing recognized judges to Australia or by going abroad to be judged. Joan Sutherland is, of course, in a class by herself. Popular singers like Helen Reddy and rock groups like the Bee-Gees and The Little River Band are household words around much of the world. Movies like *Picnic at Hanging Rock* and *My Brilliant Career* have stood up against the best of Hollywood or London. And, like any study of post-industrial society, this book owes a considerable debt to the path-breaking work of another Australian, economist Colin Clark.[1]

Despite the complacency of their social climate, some Australian businessmen long to expand their markets and product lines. The Australian wine industry deserves credit for a double success — not only for the quality of its products, but also for the marketing skill that enabled it to interest a predominantly Protestant and predominantly beer-drinking society in wine. Even those Australians who feel they must go abroad to excel — to rise to standards not insisted upon in the smaller society where they grew up — are examples of an attitude of striving that is not as dormant as much contemporary social commentary would suggest. The well-known efforts of those new Australians who, with help from their wives and children, run a milk-bar during the day and drive a taxi at night also exemplify a striving attitude, which adds to and complements the traditional. In short, Australians who continue to strive for greater achievements are by no means the endangered species they are often assumed to be. Indeed, the continuing impact of a striving attitude will probably be strong enough to offset somewhat the otherwise strong tendencies to take affluence for granted.

The attitudes labelled no worries, mateship and egalitarianism, and protect-my-corner have visible and important effects on Australian life today. Along with various economic pressures that point to a business-as-usual future, these attitudes suggest that Australians are not about to galvanize themselves into a crash program that would produce a measurably higher rate of economic growth than that of most other developed countries. At the same time, a striving attitude acts to counter these easy-going tendencies; without pushing Australia into economic dynamism, it should make a business-as-usual future more likely than a premature adoption of post-industrial values, and increase the likelihood that a "reformed" protectionist future might be sought.

No business-as-usual future can last indefinitely: indeed, the very concept is ambiguous. Since any course of events leads to a certain amount of evolution, even a future continuing on current lines has many kinds of changes built into it. If at some point any single change becomes large enough, or the evolutionary process itself becomes large enough, then a projection that fails to take account of such changes can no longer be called business-as-usual. For example, if some obvious discontinuity occurred, such as an unexpected war or an overwhelming natural calamity (like the 1974 cyclone in Darwin), then the course of events after that unexpected occurrence would no longer deserve the name business-as-usual. On the other hand, this alternative does not exclude evolutionary changes, at least for a while. The test of what is evolutionary and what is discontinuous is to some degree arbitrary, but not so arbitrary as to be meaningless. Despite the difficulty of distinguishing among different degrees of twilight, one can still distinguish between night and day.

Eventually, then, a business-as-usual alternative has to evolve one way or another. If Australian society were suddenly to become much wealthier than it is today, this increased wealth would probably create much stronger pressure to move to a premature post-industrial future. Correspondingly, if a business-as-usual alternative suddenly began to develop internal contradictions — if, for example, continued protection of obsolete manufacturing sectors became too onerous — pressure would then mount to move from business-as-usual to "reformed" protectionism.

Australia might also move toward "reformed" protectionism via a detour into a premature post-industrial alternative. In this case, it would soon be clear that the post-industrial alternative had occurred too early, much as Uruguay once assumed that it had done so well that its future was assured for the rest of history. A strong backlash might set in that, instead of bringing the society back to business-as-usual, would carry it all the way to "reformed" protectionism. Thus, when it is suggested that a business-as-usual future is likely to continue in Australia for a decade or so, this includes the possibility that there will be at least a partial evolution to some aspects of a premature post-industrial alternative, or to "reformed" protectionism, or both. By the turn of the century, Australia will in one way or another have moved away from business-as-usual — or will be forced to move away. Indeed, a relatively early attempt to move from business-as-usual to a "reformed" protectionism — or to an economically dynamic alternative — would enable Australia to have much greater control over changes the country will eventually have to make anyway.

To summarize, our basic prognosis for a business-as-usual future is that the current stagflation will continue well into the 1980s. Although a small resource boom or a number of small reforms might improve the situation, these improvements would be unlikely to have a large, sustained effect. Greatly increased strains, perhaps caused by sharply increased unemployment levels, are possible, but are also unlikely to have a large, sustained effect. Society would respond with enough countermeasures to keep them from getting out of hand.

One reason for expecting this kind of relative stability in the 1980s is that the Australian economy at the beginning of the 1970s was in a period of unquestioned boom, and the liberties that many Australians, particularly intellectuals and upper-middle class elites, felt they could take in such circumstances were much greater than now. In the current environment, by contrast, Australia faces a period of at least relative malaise: in such a period, even intellectuals and upper-middle class elites tend to act with greater restraint than during periods of boom. Although unemployment is not as serious as many Australians suggest, certain aspects of the contemporary unemployment problem are serious — indeed, serious enough, relative to the boom days of the early 1970s, to keep the system closely attuned to preventing strains from getting out of hand. The basic trend among all affluent societies is to move sooner or later towards a post-industrial future. A part of this long-term trend are the "New Emphases" of intellectuals and other upper-middle class elites, which can be expected to emerge, and to re-emerge, whenever general economic or political conditions permit. This emergence of the New Emphases is especially likely during periods of boom, but is also part of a continuing long-term trend.

A Premature Post-Industrial Australia

To describe Australia as a "post-industrial" society is in some ways to state the obvious: even people who are unfamiliar with the term have a common-sense understanding of what it means. However, as Chapter 4 argues, the concept has generally been poorly defined. If most studies of post-industrial society are classified as either exploratory or utopian, then the exploratory studies define such a society mainly in negative terms while the utopian studies describe the utopia. The exploratory studies, in other words, describe post-industrial society only in terms of what it is not — namely, that it is neither pre-industrial nor

industrial; the concept is not defined in terms of what such a
society actually is, or would be. For example, in a recent study of
Japan, we could do no more than describe "post-industrial" in
the following terms:

> It goes beyond conventional ideas of an industrial society — that is,
> . . . it is not restricted much, if at all, by the requirements of creating
> and maintaining an industrial sector. The reason is not that the out-
> put of industry is unimportant, but rather that furnishing the inputs
> and controlling the unintended external effects will become so easy
> to manage.[2]

In simpler terms, the benefits of industrialization make life easier
than it used to be.

Australia, as an industrialized country, is clearly enjoying these
benefits in contrast, say, to its nearest neighbours, Papua New
Guinea and Indonesia. The contrast is also visible if one recalls
the conditions of life in pre-industrial Australia: more than half
the population was still in legal or physical servitude, or born into
families that had come to Australia in such servitude; the main
means of transportation was by ox-cart; and supplies were subject
to loss or delay: in New South Wales, "on 8 March 1794 the very
last provisions were emptied from the stores, and six hours later
an English storeship was seen from the headland."[3]

If an industrialized country can by definition produce enough
surplus product to make such harsh conditions of pre-industrial
life a thing of the past, then by implication a post-industrial
society should continue this trend. However, even a fully post-
industrial society will include some aspects of the traditional production system, and, more broadly, some traditional values. Not
everyone can be a member of the joy-love-spontaneity culture;
not everyone can drop out. The question, of course, is how to
balance the old and the new. No country, even one as well-
endowed as Australia, can yet be described as fully post-
industrial: for the moment even the most "post-industrial-like"
society is in no more than an emerging stage.

Step-by-step, ever-continuing surplus production brings a decline in the utility of that same production. Under current and
likely future conditions, as the wealth of a wealthy nation

increases, the marginal utility of each extra increment of wealth diminishes. Like an individual who must choose between extra work or extra leisure, a nation's attitude toward work and leisure will change over time, and must constantly be reassessed in the light of evolving conditions. In one of the earliest and best discussions of some of the issues raised by the accumulation of wealth, John Maynard Keynes described the problem in the following way:

> ... the economic problem, the struggle for subsistence, always has been hitherto the primary, most pressing problem of the human race. If the economic problem is solved, mankind will be deprived of its traditional purpose.
>
> Will this be of a benefit? If one believes at all in the real values of life, the prospect at least opens up the possibility of benefit. Yet I think with dread of the readjustment of the habits and instincts of the ordinary man, bred into him for countless generations, which he may be asked to discard within a few decades ... thus for the first time since his creation man will be faced with his real, his permanent problem — how to use his freedom from pressing economic cares, how to occupy his leisure, which science and compound interest will have won for him, to live wisely and agreeably and well.[4]

Keynes' fears may or may not be justified: for the world in general, it is much too early to tell, but if Keynes could visit Australia today, he would probably think his dread was justified. To improve the condition of life through industrialization is one thing: it is quite a different notion to assume, like some Australians, that the necessity for work itself is already so minimal as to be almost eliminated. Again, the question is one of degree: to continue working to a level that might seem satisfactory by contemporary standards in Australia, but that falls increasingly short of the performance of most other countries, is, eventually, to risk conquest or domination by others, or internal stagnation.

To be sure, all developed countries are moving toward a post-industrial society. Enough data already exist to suggest that in time most of even the poorest of today's societies will reach industrialization by one path or another and eventually become post-industrial. At that point, which an earlier Hudson Institute study guessed would be reached in two hundred years, all societies would be rich by today's standards and by the standards of history.[5] Problems of absolute poverty, as traditionally perceived, would be eliminated, much in the manner that Keynes envisaged. Unlike Keynes, we do not look forward to this new era "with dread", but rather with the same guarded optimism that we consider the most effective attitude to take toward many current issues. As the earlier study concluded:

> The post-industrial world we foresee will be one of increased abundance, and thus hopefuly of reduced competition; it will be one of greater travel and contact, and thus possibly one of diminished differences among its peoples. But it will also be one of enormous power to direct and manipulate both man and nature; and thus its great issues will still be the very questions that confront us now, though enlarged in range and magnitude: Who will direct and manipulate, and to what ends?[6]

Thus, we do not assert that the elimination of problems of absolute poverty, as traditionally perceived, will eliminate problems of relative poverty, or related problems of wealth, power, and status. We do believe that a post-industrial world will be able to solve problems of absolute poverty in a way that is not possible today, and that problems of relative poverty, wealth, power, and status will probably be dealt with as satisfactorily as they are today, possibly more so.

For Australia, then, the question is less one of whether, but rather of how, to become a post-industrial society. If the process of economic development is taking the form of a gradually declining rate of economic growth for the world as a whole, Australia (or any country) still faces the question of where it would like to be on this curve of average world growth. Would it prefer to be roughly where it is today, very much in the upper range of a per capita income scale of countries making up the overall average? If so, how willing is it to make sacrifices to attain that? Alternatively, since Australia's relative ranking in per capita income among developed countries has been falling since the 1890s, would it be content to continue letting other countries pass it by, as long as it remained in absolute terms about as well off as it is today, or possibly a bit better off? In other words, would Australians prefer to be richer than most other people, without necessarily being richer than everyone else? Or would they be willing to let not only the French, Germans, Canadians, and Japanese pass them, but eventually also the Koreans, Chinese, Mexicans, and Brazilians as well — again, as long as they could remain, in absolute terms, as well off as they are today? Here, too, the real question is: how much would Australia be willing to sacrifice for how much gain?

An early post-industrial Australia would probably pay particular attention to social welfare and leisure, as distinguished from other kinds of post-industrial activities. Not only are increased welfare and leisure a natural part of such a society, but they are the very aspects which Australians themselves chose to emphasize during the early-to-mid-1970s, when the economy first became rich enough to be at least partially post-industrial. Australia is also — at least at the moment — the kind of society that would not immediately challenge the assumption of a "fixed pie", and adopt a growth-oriented solution. By contrast, countries in the neo-Confucian cultural area — Japan, South Korea, Taiwan, Hong Kong, Singapore, China itself, and probably, in due course, Vietnam and North Korea as well — certainly prefer a growth-oriented solution.

Thus, the strong emphasis on welfare and leisure that emerged in Australia in the 1970s may have been premature. If the emphasis that was then placed on living well in the immediate future were to continue more or less unchanged, it would leave Australia with a lower per capita income than either Japan or the U.S., its most likely trading partners and the two countries with which it will almost certainly have the most extensive dealings. Although the growth rates of all developed countries, including Japan and the U.S., are probably already tapering off in a long-term sense, Australia's rate of growth under a premature post-industrial alternative would taper off so soon that it would eventually flatten out at a much lower level than either of its closest partners. Roughly speaking, Australia would be in the same position vis-à-vis Japan and the U.S. that New Zealand already is with Australia, or that Ireland has traditionally been with Britain — that is, poorer and consequently looked down upon. Under this alternative, Australians might still feel sufficiently well-off in a material sense not to worry about the gap in their standard of living compared to Japan or the U.S., but they could hardly feel as militarily, politically, and psychologically secure as they do today.

Moreover, in qualitative terms, the kind of welfare-and-leisure-oriented society that Australians began to favour in the 1970s would lead to a more restricted post-industrial society than either the U.S. or Japan, and probably many other countries as well, would eventually have. In contrast to earlier societies, a post-industrial society provides its citizens with a much greater range of choice of lifestyles. Here, Keynes was right — man in a post-industrial world will have greater freedom, at least from economic burdens in the traditional sense of the term, though he will also face the challenge of deciding what to do with that increased freedom. Many argue that mankind should no longer have to maintain as high a level of economic growth as in the period of industrialization, and that a conscious choice can now be made in favour of increased welfare and leisure, rather than continually deferring gratifications for the sake of some ephemeral future. We agree, at least in principle, in that we consider the basic long-term trend toward a post-industrial society both probable and desirable.

The issue, however, is still one of degree: if current trends make some sort of post-industrial Australia likely, what sort should today's Australians aim for, and at what rate? Should a post-industrial society be allowed to develop "naturally", or should the development of some aspects be slowed down, and if so, how much? For example, with regard to the U.S., a slower drift away from traditional values would be preferable, even though the drift itself is recognized as inevitable. Australia has ranked among the wealthiest of nations since the late 1800s, and played a role in world affairs far out of proportion to its relatively small population; given this heritage, how much wealth, and what kind of role, does Australia wish to seek in the future? Some post-industrial societies might begin using their economic surplus, not only for increased welfare and leisure, but also, say, to venture forth into outer space: would Australian society be incomplete if it failed to provide opportunities for Australians to choose other such aspects of a post-industrial society, along with the increased welfare and increased leisure? To rephrase the question more precisely — since, with a small population, Australia is bound to have difficulty providing its citizens with every option provided in the larger countries of the world — would Australian society be remiss if it failed to provide its citizens with a greater, rather than a lesser, number of choices, relative to those available in other emerging post-industrial societies?

One could answer this last question with a few equally rhetorical counter-questions — how much greater, how high is up, or how much is enough? The point, of course, is not to try to draw precise lines, or to describe in the abstract exactly what kind of a post-industrial society Australia should aim for. It is important for as many Australians as possible to consider this general question of degree, partly because it seems to have been overlooked in other recent discussions of the future of Australia, and partly because trade-offs between the present and the future, between consumption and investment, are among the central issues facing mankind in general, and the developed countries in particular. The question seems especially relevant to Australia, a predominantly Western society, located in a predominantly non-Western part of the globe which shows every sign of growing at higher rates than any other part.

"Reformed" Protectionism

Australians have been talking about a "reformed" protectionist alternative for at least fifteen years. Three government-sponsored study groups — the Vernon Committee in 1965, the Jackson Committee in 1975, and the Crawford Committee in 1979 — all recommended a gradual reduction in Australia's traditionally high levels of protection for the manufacturing industry.[7] A government White Paper drafted in 1977 in response to the Jackson Committee took basically this same position.[8] Earlier, the reorganization of the Tariff Board into the Industries Assistance Commission was undertaken with this same goal in mind.

The Whitlam government actually reduced the level of tariff protection, though the effects of this step were soon eclipsed by exchange rate changes in Australia and elsewhere. Numerous academic and privately-sponsored studies — notably, in recent years, a conference of leading economists in 1977 at Salamander Bay, N.S.W. and a series of articles in 1978 by Peter Robinson of *The National Times* — also advocated a reduction in the level of protection and a more entrepreneurial approach to manufacturing, especially toward potential export markets.[9] This proliferation of similar views suggests that a consensus exists (at least among people who have studied the subject), not only on the economic distortions caused by protectionism, but also on the dangers of continuing adherence to it. In general, however, this consensus has not been translated into policy; the short-term political costs of reducing protectionism have evidently been considered too high.

The consistent failure of Australian political leaders to respond to this repeated criticism of protection raises the question of whether the analysis itself is unduly pessimistic. Or, if the analysis is more or less accurate, perhaps its implications have to be carried through to their logical conclusion — in other words, Australia's economic condition may have to deteriorate much more than it has already before the corrective steps suggested in the analysis can be taken. We take a position between these two extremes. We see a business-as-usual alternative leading to an increasingly inefficient, uncompetitive, and isolated Australia; but we do not expect this to produce truly disastrous consequences — except perhaps in the long run, after twenty years or more. Further, a policy-induced movement away from business-as-usual, toward either a "reformed" protectionism or an economically dynamic Australia, could make a great deal of difference to the kind of country Australia becomes in the twenty-first century. In other words, we agree with the general thrust of the analyses of protectionism that have been presented over the last fifteen years, but we have noticed that the dire consequences often forecast if the recommendations were ignored have not, in fact, occurred. Many trends that these reports characterized as detrimental to the economic future of the country have continued as before, thereby making matters worse, but Australia's relative isolation has kept the starkest consequences still some years away. This probably explains why these reports have fallen largely on deaf ears: they have lost some of their credibility because their dire predictions have not materialized. Hence, the problem for the ensuing two decades, to the extent that it is a problem, is as much psychological as economic.

The basic thrust of a "reformed" protectionist approach is to retain certain benefits that protectionism provides — most of them non-economic — while lowering the costs. If Australia's protectionist policies were more selective, more geared to a policy that explicitly sought to keep some degree of protectionism for the sake of certain explicitly justified long-term benefits, then the cost of a less-than-efficient allocation of resources would be more obvious, and therefore presumably more controllable.

Australians may well want to maintain a manufacturing industry — even one that is less-than-efficient in the free-market sense — on social, political, and psychological grounds, rather than for strictly economic reasons. In an industrial or emerging post-industrial era, a major country needs some manufacturing capabilities to be, in a sense, "complete". By its very nature, manufacturing helps to maintain a generalized technological capability and a mobilization base in the event of an external military threat. Just as virtually all industrial countries justify subsidies to their agricultural sectors on non-economic grounds, the strongest argument for protecting some manufacturing industry in an emerging post-industrial era is explicitly non-economic. But to minimize the economic costs, the protection of manufacturing that does exist should be directed toward explicitly long-term as well as short-term goals.

Although Australians only add up to a small country in terms of population, they have traditionally thought of themselves as a large country as well — indeed, as a continent. For this reason, many would be willing to pay for a certain amount of manufacturing capability, particularly if the costs were explicitly outlined, explicitly controllable, and explicitly directed toward long-term goals. This would contrast with the kind of protectionism Australia now maintains, in which both the goals and the gains are explicitly short-term, but the costs are implicit and increasing. Again, the issue is one of degree: not between protectionism and free-trade, but among different degrees of protection for different mixes of economic and non-economic goals. The test of effectiveness should still be the free market — there being no better test — but modifications to a free-trade version of the market system should be evaluated in the light of their long-term, rather than short-term, effects.

For example, if Australia were explicitly to eschew the use of quotas on the grounds that any quota in effect admits that a 100 per cent tariff, or more, is unable to protect a domestic industry from imports, then the economy would almost certainly gain a lot more than it would lose. A higher-than-100 per cent tariff, or its equivalent, should be thought of as too great a cost to impose on the consumer. The point also applies to intermediate products. Australia's high degree of tariff protection has led not only to higher prices for consumer products, but also to higher prices for manufacturing inputs. This policy is ultimately self-defeating, but in the absence of obvious or prohibitive costs — and failing a politically viable alternative — the existing system has continued more or less unchanged.

The "reformed" protectionist alternative is, in effect, a classic "second best" solution — an attainable improvement rather than an unattainable ideal. The aim is to provide a greater chance that some kind of manufacturing in Australia would survive over the the medium term; even if slightly uncompetitive, it would and should be no more than slightly, rather than increasingly, uncompetitive. The test should not be between protectionism and free trade in a static or abstract sense, but between protection that becomes increasingly self-defeating over time and a "reformed" protectionism whose costs are designed to be self-correcting over time.

Most recent Australian discussions of structural adjustment in manufacturing have focused on an insoluble chicken/egg question — or at least what is perceived to be a chicken/egg question. Although the need for adjustments is acknowledged, the idea persists that short-term unemployment prospects are too severe to permit such adjustments to be made. This notion is based in part on the idea that it is easier to make structural adjustments during a period of high growth, because people who might be laid off can generally find another job in an expanding economy. This is of course correct, and incidentally one benefit of a high growth economy. But in periods of high growth, when companies are typically doing well, neither they nor their employees face much pressure for structural adjustment. In any case, it does not follow that, because structural adjustments are painful in a low growth period, they should not be sought.

In fact, almost the only time structural adjustments are made is during periods of recession and high unemployment. Only then are employers and employees forced to face up to "reality". Employers, in particular, prefer to expand, especially into new lines of business, during periods when they feel a recession is about to end — that is, when business prospects are best and the cost of labour is relatively cheap because surplus labour is left over from the recession. Correspondingly, only during periods of recession are unemployed workers willing to increase their mobility — either by taking jobs they previously would not consider, or simply by being more willing to move. The notion that an economy is unable to adjust during a period of high unemployment — particularly if it leads to greater protectionism for the least competitive industries — not only impedes adjustments that are a logical part of any economic system (particularly a free-market economy), but it actually makes the situation progressively worse.

There are times when a patient is too weak from a secondary problem to be treated for a major problem, although the prevalence of such occasions is greatly exaggerated. However, there is never a right time to inflict pain on a patient if one is measuring only the short-term effects of the pain *per se* and ignoring the long-term benefits of a proposed treatment. This is particularly true in situations where the patient is making the choice — when, for example, the doctor does not consider the problem urgent enough to declare the operation mandatory. In economic policy, it is one thing for the impersonal forces of the market to dictate changes, and quite another to rely on policy-induced changes that require self-inflicted pain in the short-term. Precisely because the market is so impersonal — in effect so ruthless — complaints about its being unjust are misplaced. On its own impersonal terms, the market is just; it treats everyone harshly. But if politicians or public servants are faced with the prospect of inflicting pain as a conscious decision for which they will have to take responsibility, they customarily argue that the time is not right to do so. The earlier reluctance of the Australian government to raise domestic oil prices to world levels illustrates this point. And from the viewpoint of the politicians and public servants themselves, though not from the viewpoint of society as a whole, this reluctance is understandable.

A "reformed" protectionist approach, as distinguished from business-as-usual, can only be achieved if politicians, public servants, and in turn the general public are prepared to act on the basis of a long-term program in spite of the recognized short-term costs of such a program. This means that measures should be designed to provide long-term benefits, rather than to avoid short-term costs. The short-term costs can be mitigated to some degree by long-term planning. Most of the measures Australia has so far taken to reform its protectionist approach to manufacturing have been designed primarily to minimize short-term costs, with only incidental attention to long-term benefits. In the sense used here, "reformed" protectionism would reverse this emphasis in favour of greater consideration of the long-term. While any such mixture of short and long-term criteria is obviously a compromise, its aim is to attain some improvements over a continuation of business-as-usual. A "reformed" protectionist approach that explicitly justified protection on non-economic, rather than economic, grounds would have the twin effects of providing justifiable reasons and of measuring economic costs in a way that would enable the public to decide more clearly how much protectionism it is willing to pay for.

Economic Dynamism

To reach its present level of wealth, Australia must have had a dynamic economy at various times in the past, most recently in the 1960s. For this reason alone, one might assume that it has the potential for similarly dynamic periods in the future. Yet the idea of economic dynamism is out of fashion in Australia today: what we earlier labelled the striving attitude seems overshadowed by the no worries and protect-my-corner attitudes. Furthermore, an economically dynamic Australia would be more than simply a modification of "reformed" protectionism. In a "reformed" protectionist alternative, Australia would make various improvements on business-as-usual to enable a system not too far removed from current lines to remain relatively effective for a longer period of time. In an economically dynamic Australia, the goal is to transform the country, to seek and achieve a much higher per capita income, which in turn would support a further economic and cultural flowering well beyond anything Australia has achieved to date.

Because the atmosphere of the 1960s is so recent, it provides a useful analogy to draw upon. Although the mining boom is usually emphasized, it was only a part of a much broader "Australia boom" — in manufacturing, construction, education and culture. Like all boom periods, the 1960s led to a day of reckoning. Some would link the soberness of the 1970s to excess inflation, others to excess government, still others to the Vietnam war, as a manifestation of inflated ambition. But almost no one — including critics on the left, who emphasize alleged inequities that developed in the 1960s, or those on the right, who emphasize alleged distortions — would favour a return to the Australia of the early 1950s. In other words, even advocates of a relatively stagnant Australia do not favour one as stagnant as that.

The Sydney Opera House, which many Australians take for granted today, is perhaps the most visible example of the kind of striving attitude that grew in the late fifties and blossomed in the sixties. Certainly it is more widely known around the world than any other examples. Stunning in its conception — the idea that the harbour should have an opera house — and subsequently in the design that was chosen, it has become the very symbol of the best in contemporary Australia. Moreover, choosing the design on the basis of a worldwide competition constituted a complete reversal of the traditional relationship between Australia and the world; instead of going abroad to achieve recognition, Australians invited the world to Sydney. And what an occasion it became! Still, the project had its detractors. Because of the delays and vast cost over-runs, the friction between the Danish designer, Joern Utzon, and the authorities, and the still inadequate acoustics, the Opera House is an instance of the difficulties that are encountered in any ambitious project — the possibilities of disaster as well as success, of reach exceeding grasp. Despite these imperfections and difficulties, very few Australians would feel that the Opera House has not made Sydney and Australia a better place.

This example — the pluses and the minuses, and the more important positive balance between the two — can and should be generalized. Indeed, were it not for the current strength of the no worries and protect-my-corner attitudes, the maxim, "nothing ventured, nothing gained", would seem too obvious to mention. The very need to emphasize the positive side of a striving attitude is itself a measure of how much Australian society takes its past for granted, and assumes that its future is assured.

To the degree that pressure builds up to force Australians away from business-as-usual, they will still have to choose one path or another and seek to move toward it. An economically dynamic Australia is one alternative to an early emphasis on a welfare and leisure-oriented post-industrial society, or to a "reformed" protectionism. A major difference between economic dynamism and these other alternatives is the degree of wealth that future generations would have available to support the choices they would then be able to make. Economic dynamism has its costs, of course, notably in decreased consumption for the sake of increased investment. It provides less anow in return for a greater range of choice in the future.

The surplus wealth generated by economic dynamism can be measured in two ways: a quantitative estimate of tangible wealth, such as the book value of the Opera House building, or a qualitative, intangible, and aesthetic evaluation of such an accomplishment, such as the inspiration the Opera House provides even to school children who may never have seen the building. Because the Opera House exists, being Australian has more meaning. One might also make comparisons among various cities of Europe.

During the Italian Renaissance, the cities of Venice, Florence, and Rome experienced a great burst of economic dynamism. Paris and London underwent similar periods of development in the seventeenth to nineteenth centuries. Looking back from 1980, one sees clearly that the investments made at that time continue to reap enormous benefits for all of these cities, and that the different degrees of investment since then have made a difference to future generations. Had such investments not been made — that is, had Italy, France, and Britain never followed policies of economic dynamism — where would these countries and cities be today? For that matter, what kind of country would Australia be today if Britain had not been a dynamic, expansive power in the eighteenth and nineteenth centuries?

The underlying purpose of economic dynamism, then, is more positive than negative, more to seek achievements for their own sake than merely to fend off challenges. If some Australians believe economic dynamism is worth seeking, they must still face the question of how to go about it (along with the subordinate question of how to go about it with less frustration than in the construction of the Opera House). Nowadays, when the stimulus of territorial expansion that was characteristic of the nineteenth century is no longer a realistic option — at least in plausible projections of international relations — economic dynamism can best be achieved through the efficiences generated by a market economy and supplementary government policies.

For Australia, with its enormous natural wealth, this would mean an even greater emphasis on exporting agricultural and mineral resources, and correspondingly less emphasis on the kinds of manufacturing Australian has traditionally had. Australia could still maintain some degree of manufacturing, but not the broad-based, old-fashioned, uncompetitive industry of the past. If efficiency is the criterion, Australian manufacturing would have to become more specialized, more technological, and/or more capital-intensive, that is, more oriented to export markets, mainly in the Asia-Pacific region. Instead of maintaining a protected manufacturing sector that is increasingly less supportable over the long term, Australia under this alternative would shift to a manufacturing sector that becomes competitive as it develops, and maintains its competitiveness through the medium and the long term. The efficiencies of the market that force obsolete industries to go out of business also bring new businesses into existence, and do so to a greater degree than typically happens in a more protected economy. The uncertainties of the market are one reason for its dynamism: uncertainty leads to unexpected losses, but — and this is the point that many Australians seem to miss — it leads to unexpected gains as well. In short, economic dynamism offers greater risks in the short term — and a requirement to work harder — but promises much greater gain in the medium and long term.

An economically dynamic Australia would probably also require a substantial increase in the current rate of immigration. An expanding labour force is usually a prerequisite to, rather than a consequence of, expanded investment. A loose labour market encourages new investment, and such investment can continue for a longer period of time if the labour market remains loose, or is kept loose by an increase in the supply of labour. Moreover, as long as investment continues to expand, a loose labour market need not hold down wages; profits and wages can both go up. In a country like Australia, where 61 per cent of the population lives in five state capitals, and where a strong sense of regionalism has impeded labour mobility, an increase in the rate of immigration is almost the only way to keep the labour market expanding at a rate sufficient to avoid inflationary pressures. Also, new arrivals are psychologically more suited to an economically dynamic Australia than native-born or even first-generation Australians. Typically, the newly-arrived migrant is eager for training, employment and, most importantly, advancement.

Australians often remark that, since they come from a country with a small population, their influence on the world can only be small, and that Australia can only follow, rather than lead, world trends. At the same time, Australians take great pride when one of their number does achieve world recognition, from a base in Australia or as an expatriate. Indeed, Australians sometimes say that the country is too small to make an impact, but at the same time complain about being underrated and ignored by the world. This plaintiveness perhaps stems in part from an attitude of mateship and egalitarianism, that is, to appear to be striving too hard is to violate the social order. Yet Australia has achieved its current standard of living, and has done so on the basis of something besides sheer luck. With more emphasis on economic dynamism, the "closet strivers" might come out of their closets — or, more significantly, many citizens might be inspired to strive — and leave an even greater mark than they have so far on both Australia and the world.

Unlikely Alternatives

The four alternatives outlined above do not, of course, take account of all the possibilities that might arise for Australia over the next two decades or beyond. One might consider other possibilities, either to insure against thinking too much along current lines, or simply to test one's imagination, particularly about possible "disaster" scenarios. Some other alternatives might include the following:

1. **A nationalistic, isolationist Australia**, in which the country sought to emphasize its isolation, not only from Asia but even from various post-industrial trends taking hold in North America and Europe. One version of this alternative could be a self-contained, static, and internally stable Australia, but held together, like Tokugawa Japan, only by an extremely authoritarian government. Contemporary Australians would presumably object to choosing this alternative if they recognized that it would require an authoritarian government.

2. **A strongly socialist Australia**, in which the country sought to change its mixed-market economic system to one with an even greater degree of income equality than is already the case, and a greater degree of central planning and public ownership of the means of production. To build morale, a government that tried to implement this program would perhaps argue that such a strongly socialist Australia would constitute the closest approximation to utopia that mankind had yet developed; it would be, the argument would run, a democratic socialist, not communist, system,

and an improvement on the democratic, but insufficiently
socialist, economies of Western Europe and North America.
Advocates of this approach might also suggest that since
Australia's isolation permits it to adopt a more strongly socialist
approach than other developed countries, it should take advantage of this isolation, follow its own path, and thereby show the
world how life could and should be lived.

3. A "small-is-beautiful" Australia, in which the population
and rate of growth were kept to minimum levels — on the
grounds that Australia's current level of "good living" was acceptable to most of its citizens. Attempts to industrialize further or to
seek higher growth rates would be seen as leading only to more
"plunder", pollution, and a decreasing quality of life of the sort
associated with industrialization in much contemporary social
commentary. Under this alternative, the environment would be
sanctified and almost inviolable.

4. Constitutional reform, in which the emphasis is placed not on
long-term efficiency or on prospects for future growth but on one
particular version of social justice in the short term. Proponents
would argue that social justice in Australia cannot be achieved in
the context of the existing constitution, which they see as biased
against the Labor party. To build morale, some advocates of this
approach would also seek to establish a republic, abolishing the
link between the British monarchy and Australia on the grounds
that only an Australian head-of-state could bring true self-respect
to the country.

5. An "arranged marriage" with Japan, in which the argument
is made that the easiest, and therefore most profitable,
choice for Australia is simply to supply natural resources, particularly energy resources, to the largest nearby market, Japan.
According to this argument, Australia would get a steady income,
but could run its own society as it pleased, while Japan would get
a steady stream of resources and in turn could run its society as it
pleased. This alternative would amount to an Australian version
of a Japanese-style marriage. Both spouses would be indissolubly
linked, and would complement each other, but without having

much contact outside the specific context of this complementarity.

6. "**Colonization**", in which the country's resources are considered so valuable that some other country or countries would seek to dominate Australia, directly or indirectly, in order to guarantee themselves access to these resources. One can imagine, for example, that some time in the twenty-first century China and Japan might become rivals for influence elsewhere in Asia, and that a resource-rich Australia would be one object of their rivalry. The word "colonization" is in quotation marks to leave open the exact form by which China or Japan, or some group of countries allied with one or the other, might try to implement a policy of dominating Australia.

A common trend of isolationism runs through several of these unlikely alternatives. In a sense, this isolationism reflects not only an extreme version of a protect-my-corner attitude, but also an attempt to create what proponents of such alternatives would contend was a "better Australia". It is clear, however, that any future Australia would have great difficulty becoming more isolated than it is now, at least if it were seeking to preserve current Australian living standards.

All of these possibilities — both the more likely and the less likely — have a virtually infinite number of permutations which could all be discussed if one wanted to elaborate theories for their own sake. But to promote discussion of the future of Australia among as wide a public as possible, some things have to be omitted, and we have chosen to omit a detailed discussion of scenarios that we consider really improbable. Instead, we concentrate on the four alternatives that we consider the most likely choices for Australia over the next ten to twenty years.

These likely alternatives present a relatively circumscribed, but also distinctly different, set of choices. No one alternative is radically different from the other three in its consequences for the rest of this century, but each has very different implications for Australia in the twenty-first century. Moreover, in the real world, these alternatives will be mixed together. Some people will be more "post-industrial" than others, some more "striving" than others. The problem of which alternative to choose is almost a textbook example of the role of values in rational decision-making. If Australians as a group place a higher value on the short rather than the long term — on consumption in the present rather than investment in future — they will clearly prefer either a business-as-usual or a premature post-industrial alternative, and leave consideration of the longer term to future generations. If, on the other hand, Australians agree that the country's current relative prosperity is unlikely to last in the absence of specific steps to make it last longer, they will prefer, as a matter of logic, either "reformed" protectionism or economic dynamism.

   In any discussion of alternative futures, there is a tendency to assume that one course of action is morally or philosophically superior to another. While this may be so, this problem is separate from the reasons for "reformed" protectionism or economic dynamism mentioned above. A decision to adopt either of these alternatives can simply be based on cost/benefit criteria. When, for example, the idea for the Opera House was first conceived, its proponents and opponents did not assess the idea on primarily moral or philosophical grounds but on a practical basis. Such an approach is relatively easy to take in the case of a single project like the Opera House, but is much more difficult to maintain as the scope of the question under consideration grows. If one is discussing something as broad as the future of Australia, the normative aspects become so overwhelming that the practical considerations — the pros and cons of various approaches — are often lost. One purpose of this book is to describe, as clearly as possible, the consequences of various alternative future for Australia, and to separate this discussion of the pros and cons of different alternatives from their normative aspects. The question of which alternative is preferable on moral or philosophical grounds presumably depends in part on the feasibility of various alternatives.

Notes

1. See, for example, *The Conditions of Economic Progress*, 3rd ed. (New York: St Martin's Press, 1957).
2. Herman Kahn and Thomas Pepper, *The Japanese Challenge: The Success and Failure of Economic Success* (Sydney: Harper & Row, 1979), p. 30.
3. Geoffrey Blainey, *The Tyranny of Distance* (Melbourne: Sun Books, 1966), p. 48.
4. "Economic Possibilities for our Grandchildren", (1930), reprinted in J.M. Keynes, *Essays in Persuasion* (New York: W.W. Norton, 1963), pp. 366-67.
5. Herman Kahn, William Brown, and Leon Martel, *The Next 200 Years* (New York: William Morrow and Company, 1976), *passim*.
6. Ibid., p. 226.
7. The Vernon Committee published its findings under the title, *Report of the Committee of Economic Enquiry* (Canberra: Australian Government Publication Service). The Jackson Committee published its finding under the title, *Policies for Development of Manufacturing Industry* (Canberra: AGPS). The Crawford Committee published its findings as the report of the *Study Group on Structural Adjustment* (Canberra: AGPS).
8. White Paper on Manufacturing Industry (Canberra: AGPS).
9. The proceedings from the conference at Salamander Bay are summarized in Wolfgang Kasper and Thomas G. Parry, eds., *Growth, Trade and Structural Change in an Open Australian Economy* (Kensington, N.S.W.: Centre for Applied Economic Research, University of New South Wales, 1978). The series of articles by Robinson were published weekly in *The National Times* from 5 August 1978 through 23 September 1978, and published subsequently under the title, *The Crisis in Australian Capitalism* (Fitzroy, Vic.: VCTA Publishing Pty Ltd, 1978).

TWO

A Historical and World Context

As the 1960s ended and talk of an expansive new decade dominated discussions of the early 1970s, few anticipated the enormous economic, social, and political changes that were soon to
occur. The sudden end to an extended period of high economic
growth in the developed nations (both capitalist and communist)
was marked by the emergence of, among other things: an
increase in oil prices (nominally introduced and sustained by
OPEC), double-digit inflation on a global scale, numerous structural imbalances, and various changes in social values, all of
which gave rise to a business climate dramatically different from
the previous twenty-five years.

Many discussions of the 1980s assume, like their counterparts
ten years before, that this new decade is very likely to repeat the
experiences of the recent past, that is, there will be continued low
economic growth, continuedupward pressure on energy prices,
and continued double-digit inflation (or something close to it) as
a "norm". We disagree. Although we do not expect a return to
the average growth rates characteristic of the period between
1947 and 1973, we do foresee a good possibility for gradual and
creative adjustment and innovation as the decade proceeds.
There are also many possibilities for disaster, but little likelihood
that there will be just more of the same. The rise in energy prices
that occurred during the 1970s is unlikely to continue during the
1980s. Similarly, though inflation rates will initially subside only
grudgingly, they are most unlikely to remain at their current
levels for long, at least in the developed countries. Over time, the

adjustments that are made to recent energy price increases and high inflation rates will exert a cumulative influence on the course of events, leading eventually to higher growth rates than those evident at the beginning of the decade.[1] On the other hand, the 1980s will probably witness a series of political and military challenges to the international system, in particular to the position of the United States as the more dominant of the two superpowers.

Throughout the 1970s, most of us at Hudson Institute argued that the long-term prospects for mankind were probably favourable, or at least more likely to be favourable than unfavourable. In two studies of worldwide economic prospects,[2] and in various studies of specific issues or countries in the context of these two general studies,[3] we usually took a "guarded optimist" position: meaning that, while various problems would occur, there were practical measures that could — and probably would — be taken to deal with such problems more or less effectively. To be sure, much of this "guarded optimism" depends on a restoration of the U.S.'s willingness and ability to play a genuine leadership role. The longer such a recovery — economic, military, and political — is delayed, the less a "guarded optimist" position is justified, because political and military challenges to the existing international system would still be growing.

Take, for example, the general world reaction to the initial U.S. response to events in late 1979 in Iran and Afghanistan. Other countries, regardless of ideology or alliance position, received an impression of continued American weakness, vacillation and even helplessness. Under Prime Minister Fraser, Australia clearly stood out from other countries because of its pleas for a stronger, more unified stand against both terrorism and attempts by the Soviet Union to extend its influence. The Fraser government also announced an increased defence program and other foreign policy measures of the sort it was urging other countries to adopt. The reaction to these moves within Australia ranged from opposition to bemusement. Opponents of the Liberal/ Country party coalition and much of the press showed little enthusiasm for Fraser's announced goal of a broadly-based anti-Soviet campaign or his contention that Australia, though a small country, had a role to play — indeed, a duty to take part — in such a campaign. Among both supporters and opponents of the government, there was an all-too-evident tendency to treat these moves as clever election-year tactics that would go over well with a latently patriotic, anti-communist Australian public or even as simply another example of the sort of rhetoric that politicians like to indulge in.

This may well have been among Fraser's motivations. But under current circumstances, it is not as hard for us to take seriously the idea that an Australian prime minister could be playing a significant world role as it is for Australians. Whether it seems plausible or not, Prime Minister Fraser's meeting with President Carter in late January 1980, and his subsequent visit to Western Europe and return to Washington, seem to have provided significant support to attempts by the Carter administration to move in a direction useful for the U.S., Australia, and all other non-communist countries. One could wish the U.S. were so strong that it did not have to depend so much on support from smaller powers like Australia, but that seems to have been the situation in this case. Hence the question must be asked: what might happen if the U.S. continues to pursue military and political policies that make it almost impossible to carry out the kind of leadership role it played from 1945 to the late 1970s? Indeed, unless some recovery in U.S. policy occurs rather soon, a "guarded pessimist" position would become increasingly justified, at least from the viewpoint of those who would like the U.S. to remain the strongest single power in the world.

Without pursuing further the details of current U.S. policies, this chapter outlines a "guarded optimist" version of an economic and political context for Australia over the next ten to twenty years, and beyond. It is assumed that, as a relatively minor power, Australia is more affected by the world economic and political context than the rest of the world is affected by Australia — although this does not exclude particular ways in which Australia might influence the rest of the world.

A World Economic Context

The Great Transition

We being by describing a long-term perspective for the economic present and future. We identify two watersheds in mankind's economic history: the agricultural revolution that occurred some ten thousand years ago, and what is referred to at Hudson Institute as the Great Transition in which we are living today. There may be other watersheds yet to come, for example, a movement into space, with settlements on other celestial bodies and/or in man-made space colonies. This latter possibility, which we personally think is likely, would lead eventually to the development of new kinds of economic activities in space that would differ radically from our previous earth-bound experiences. A watershed could also come from a disastrous world war that need not destroy civilization but could certainly change it. For the moment, however, the Great Transition is considered in the context of economic growth on earth.[4]

Figure 2.1 summarizes this four hundred year Great Transition, showing it as comprising three phases: the industrial revolution, the super-industrial economy, and the emergence of a post-industrial economy. This Great Transition is often summarized as follows:

> Two hundred years ago, almost everywhere human beings were comparatively few, poor, and at the mercy of the forces of nature; two centuries hence, barring some combination of very bad luck and/or bad management, they should be, almost everywhere, numerous, rich, and largely in control of the forces of nature.

This scenario is not inevitable, but it is likely and plausible, given the data and trends that are known today. A model of much of this past and future history is embodied in the S-shaped, or logistic, curve shown on Figure 2.1. After having been a small fraction of a percent for many millennia, growth rates for world population and gross world product began to increase appreciably in the seventeenth and eighteenth centuries, and recently attained a pace which, if continued for a century or so, might

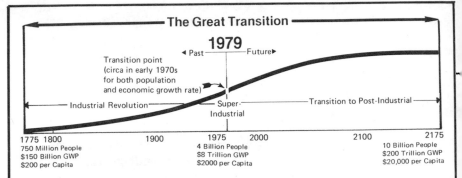

The Great Transition

1979
◀ Past ────┬──── Future ▶

Transition point
(circa in early 1970s
for both population
and economic growth rate)

◀──────── Industrial Revolution ────────▶   Super-─────   ◀──── Transition to Post-Industrial ────▶
                                             Industrial

1775 1800	1900	1975 2000	2100	2175
750 Million People		4 Billion People		10 Billion People
$150 Billion GWP		$8 Trillion GWP		$200 Trillion GWP
$200 per Capita		$2000 per Capita		$20,000 per Capita

Notes: The plot is semi-logarithmic. GWP=Gross World Product. Sums are in 1979 dollars. Figures for 1775 are approximations based on historical data; figures for 2175 are projections based on reasonable assumptions and current trends.

Pre 1775
: All societies are pre-industrial, Income Ratio (ratio of richest 10%) about 5 to 1.

1775–1875
: 100 Years for initial industrialization of North Western Europe, Japan and North America, Income Ratio goes to about 20 to 1.

1875–1950
: Emergence of mass consumption societies in Europe, Japan, and North America start of worldwide industrialization.

1950–1990
: Four decades of rapid worldwide economic and population growth; initial emergence of super-industrial economies, technological crises, and many historic transitions, e.g., inflection points in world population and perhaps gross product curves (also first steps into space).

1990–2025
: Emergence of post-industrial economies in most Western and some Neo-Confucian cultures — perhaps also in U.S.S.R. Full development of super-industrial cultures and societies in advanced countries. First signs of a worldwide maturing economy. (First serious moves to colonize space.)

2025–2175
: Worldwide slowing down in population and economic growth rates (not only in percent but also in absolute numbers). As a result it takes almost 150 years for emergence of post-industrial economies almost everywhere. (Perhaps also the establishment of an independent solar system society.) Income Ratios (on earth) 40 to 1 or less — perhaps much less.

Post 2175
: Post-industrial society either stabilizes or ossifies, or else the next development in mankind emerges.

Notes: We distinguish among economy, institutions, culture, and society as follows:

Economy: economic and technological activity.
Institutions: laws and organizations.
Culture: style, values, national character, and attitudes.
Society: the whole.

Presumably first the economy emerges, then the institutions and the culture, and finally one has a society, although one or two of these factors may greatly influence the others.

Super-Industrial Economy refers to the large size and scale of modern enterprise and the importance of its impact on the external social and physical development.
Post-Industrial Economy refers to a future very affluent economy that meets its industrial and material needs with a small percent of its work force and economic effort.

The Neo-Confucian cultures here are Japan and Singapore, and perhaps South Korea, Hong Kong, and Taiwan.

Fig. 2.1   The Great Transition

indeed lead to overwhelming problems. We believe that the average rates for both have peaked, leading to a gradual levelling-off process, which will eventually stabilize at high and sustainable levels of both population and gross world product per capita in the late twenty-first century

This slowing down in the growth of world population and gross world product will stem less from physical limitations on resources or other supply-based limits than from changes in priorities, values, and tastes — that is, from demand. In particular, priorities and values will change as people are influenced by high levels of affluence and advanced technology, and the operation of a law of diminishing returns to increased affluence — that is, by the spread of better standards of health, safety, literacy, and the like. As people become better off, they tend first to show less enthusiasm for having a large family. Eventually, they also become less interested than their parents in acquiring more material goods. In other words, the rate of increase in traditional demands tapers off and new demands arise: less restructuring of the economy and less hassle, and possibly less work and more leisure. This does not suggest, of course, that this chain of events will be smooth or automatic. On the contrary, mankind will certainly be plagued by many age-old problems for a long time to come, and will encounter many new ones along the way, some of which are unforeseeable today.

World Economic Development

Modern economic growth can be divided into four phases:[5] the first, moderately, but unprecedentedly dynamic; the second disastrous; the third, highly dynamic; and the fourth — most of which lies ahead — a troubled period which is neither fully healthy but hopefully not really sick either. Figure 2.2, based on data compiled by Angus Maddison, shows how these four periods can be distinguished by the rate and smoothness of growth in the aggregate output of sixteen Advanced Capitalist Nations (ACNs), including Australia.[6] These nations grew at an unheard of pace during *La Première Belle Epoque* (the first good era). By contrast, during *La Mauvaise Epoque* (the bad era), they grew

The Four Periods of the 20th Century

	1	**2**	**3**	**4**
Duration	1886 thru 1913 (28 years)	1914 thru 1947 (34 years)	1948 thru 1973 (26 years)	1974 thru 2000? (27 years)
Average Growth Rate of Advanced Capitalist Nations	3.3%	1.8%	4.9%	3.5%
Other Economic Growth	Russia also takes off; rest of world stagnant	Soviet Union grows 5-10%; rest of world still stagnant	Middle-income nations take off and grow 5-10%	COMECON (Soviet bloc nations) is about 4% (perhaps less) but middle-income nations continue at 5-10%
Some Outstanding Characteristics of the Period	Creation of a spectacular gap between the Advanced Capitalist nations and the rest of the world	Two world wars, the great depression, rise and fall of facism, two great communist revolutions, emergence of two super-powers	Cold war, decolonization, emergence of middle-income nations, emergence of Japan as second or third greatest economy, emergence of new class limits to growth concepts and ideologies. Many S-shaped curves reach their maximum percent growth rate	Further emergence of middle-income nations, great potential for violence and disorder, vulnerable national and world economic systems —but less than 30% of the world lives in "poor nations"
Name of Period	**La Belle Epoque** The Good Era	**La Mauvaise Epoque** The Bad Era	**La Deuxième Belle Epoque** The Second Good Era	**L'Epoque de Malaise?** The Era of Malaise?

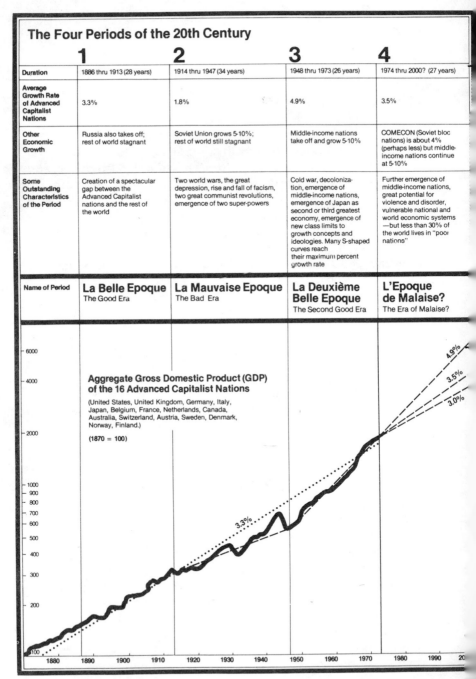

Aggregate Gross Domestic Product (GDP) of the 16 Advanced Capitalist Nations

(United States, United Kingdom, Germany, Italy, Japan, Belgium, France, Netherlands, Canada, Australia, Switzerland, Austria, Sweden, Denmark, Norway, Finland.)

(1870 = 100)

Fig. 2.2 Aggregate GDP of the Sixteen Advanced Capitalist Nations during Four Periods of Twentieth Century

only about half as rapidly. During this bad era, many disturbing
and unpleasant events took place: two world wars, several runa-
way inflations, the rise and fall of fascism, two communist
revolutions, and the Great Depression. During *La Deuxième Belle
Epoque*, the ACNs experienced extraordinarily good times,
although few people who lived through this good period were
aware of the degree of prosperity that was occurring at the time.
The reason for this is simple: if someone is healthy, this seems
normal, and he pays little attention to his good fortune, still less
to how this good fortune might look in historical perspective.

From the viewpoint of economic growth, *La Deuxième Belle
Epoque* was an extraordinarily creative and productive period.
During the twenty-six years from 1948 through 1973, growth
rates of the ACNs averaged about 5 per cent a year. This was the
first time in history that such high and sustained growth rates
were achieved. Furthermore, something even more extraordinary occurred: the rest of the world, again for the first time in
history, began to industrialize rapidly. While the ACNs grew at an
unprecedented rate during *La Première Belle Epoque*, that rate
averaged only 3.3 per cent a year, or only two-thirds of that
achieved in *La Deuxième Belle Epoque*. Furthermore, except for
Russia and a few primary producing countries, the growth rate for
the rest of the world in this first era was almost negligible, often
not even keeping up with the population growth rate.

The use of a phrase like *Belle Epoque* does not, of course, imply
that there were no problems in the ACNs, not to say the rest of
the world, during these two periods. Nor does it imply that such
epochs occurred simultaneously in all these countries. Indeed, in
some of the ACNs, particularly the United States, the deterioration in economic and social conditions that followed *La Deuxième
Belle Epoque* started in the early or mid-1960s, rather than the
early or mid-1970s. In any case, similar kinds of problems had
begun to affect almost all the advanced capitalist nations (and the
advanced communist nations as well) by the mid-1970s. For this
reason, the period beginning with 1974 may justifiably be referred to as *L'Epoque de Malaise*, at least in the sense of being less
prosperous and less dynamic than *La Deuxième Belle Epoque*.

Perhaps the single most striking characteristic of *L'Epoque de*

Malaise is that it combines relatively high unemployment, excess industrial capacity, and inflation; all three phenomena affect most ACNs today to some degree. The term "stagflation" has been coined to describe this condition, which is increasingly thought of as more or less chronic for most ACNs. A decade before, many observers would have denied that such a widespread and persistent combination of difficulties was even possible. The persistent stagflation of the current period can be attributed partly to structural[7] (including institutional) factors, but mostly to a prolonged period of unwise fiscal, monetary, and regulatory policies. However, even if these policies had been much wiser, there would still have been some degree of malaise, though presumably less widespread and persistent.

Some readers may associate this view of economic history with speculations in recent economic literature about long-term cycles associated mainly with the Russian economist Nikolai D. Kondratieff. Without endorsing any specific long-cycle analysis, we do believe that elements from various interpretations of Kondratieff's hypothesis contribute greatly to an understanding of the way in which the world economy is evolving. Indeed, the long-cycle forces at work have quite different characteristics among various ACNs, but they interact and feed on one another due to increased international interdependence.

The behaviour patterns of a typical long-cycle of activity, incorporating social, political, and psychological, as well as economic trends, might be described as follows:

Archetype Long Cycle

1. **A sobering context**. The cycle begins with stagnation and very slow growth, deterioration of plant and equipment, and little or no exploitation of new technologies or other innovations. This creates or encourages competitive situations, and most wages and other costs tend to become more competitive.

2. **Relatively cautious, disciplined behaviour**. Businessmen begin to think about opportunities, but invest mainly in low-risk ventures. Since getting a job is difficult, having a job is very

prized. High rates of saving are induced, and these may become more valued because of deflation.

3. **A turning point**. After a longer period of low investment in capital facilities, and continued slow obsolescence of existing plant, opportunities for new investment and expansion eventually open up to replace obsolete capital, and to exploit new technologies or other new opportunities,[8] creating a turning point. A slow, but general, revival of confidence in longer term prospects begins to make possible long-term investments.

4. **An expansion psychology begins to develop and full confidence is restored**. An intense search for new technologies and new opportunities, and a general willingness to replace even marginally obsolete equipment, commences. A competent, dedicated work force is still available, along with wide public and private support for economically and technologically oriented projects. There is a search for areas where investment can expand, and where a long-term view can be taken. The "creative destruction" produced by these ventures is almost always judged to be more creative than destructive.[9]

5. **A "Belle Epoque" psychology emerges**. Self-fulfilling prophecies begin to play a very important role in inspiring business investment and economic growth. People begin to take affluence and prosperity for granted, and the atmosphere becomes relaxed, even careless. Discretionary, odd, and relatively extreme behaviour begins to emerge. There is a limited emergence of anti-bourgeois, anti-materialistic attitudes and movements. Priorities and values begin to change. "Creative destruction" begins to look more destructive and less creative. Welfare and other government transfer payments increase rapidly.

6. **Confidence peaks even while extraordinary strains and excesses appear and extremist discretionary behaviour and polarization characterize society**. Demand for all kinds of commodities grows and prices rise rapidly, particularly if government officials and monetary policies encourage (or simply permit) inflation.[10] There is a boom in capital goods industries. Specula-

tion becomes rife, and is increasingly based on fashion, self-fulfilling prophecies, "discounting the hereafter", and "ponzi schemes" (that is, illusory profits paid out of capital or by income transfer). "New Class" values, especially among upper-middle class youth, appear ascendant. A peak war[11] occurs, or a similar event that goes badly. However, there is no attempt to cut losses (the dynamism and energy of society are too high). Eventually, various self-styled idealistic groups mobilize in protest against a continuation of current trends — even to the point of promoting extremist, discretionary behaviour. Indeed, being anti-establishment becomes so popular and acceptable that in many situations the roles of the pro- and con- forces may be reversed — that is, protest becomes an "establishment" value.

7. **Eventually a day of reckoning**. One or two increasingly serious recessions, or a depression, occur. Recovery is slow because of excess capacity, many new rigidities, and increasingly high social overhead costs. There is great caution among businessmen and investors, and a tendency to invest mainly for the short run (for example, to patch up old buildings rather than build new ones).[12] Eventually, either an Epoch of Malaise, or a collapse of the system (and normally of prices as well), occurs.

8. **Recovery proceeds, but erratically, with a troubled period of transition and sobering up.** Residual anti-business attitudes and institutions persist, and greatly handicap the revival of the system. Subsequently, new moods of both seriousness and cynicism, and both pessimism and hope, spread. There is as much disillusionment with the new values and attitudes as there once was with the old. Some degree of counter-reformation and a "balanced", or even perhaps excessive, emphasis on economic growth comes back. But it takes a long time to sober up — to re-establish the priorities and discipline necessary for economic growth.

This typical long swing in economic activity can be viewed as a useful way of looking at current problems. The endorsement of such a long-cycle approach is not a commitment to a particular process through which these cycles play themselves out; nor must each cycle follow the pattern of the previous cycle. The particular mechanisms at work are themselves very flexible. Society is constantly evolving, accumulating new knowledge, new technologies, and new problems. Mechanisms and modes of behaviour necessarily change, as does the ability of a society to control its own evolution. Indeed, this is one reason we feel the current period should be characterized as *L'Epoque de Malaise*, rather than *La Deuxième Mauvaise Epoque.*

Partly for simplicity and convenience, this study emphasizes the conditions that are likely to prevail in *L'Epoque de Malaise.* Other studies look at various ways in which *L'Epoque de Malaise* might break down into *La Deuxieme Mauvaise Epoque.* There are of course many ways this might happen, particularly through a further weakening of the existing international system, stemming from a further decline of American power. In such trouble spots as the Persian Gulf, the Indochina peninsula, and Central America, if current difficulties get much worse, the result would almost amount to a breakdown of the system. Even more serious would be an American neo-isolationism, in effect a backing down by the U.S. from its previous responsibilities, either because it is pushed around or because various domestic groups favour such a backing down. This set of circumstances is more consistent with a "guarded pessimist" position.

The Super-Industrial World Economy

Mankind's socio-economic development is often thought of as a progression from pre-industrial to industrial and then directly to post-industrial society. Although many of the problems of the next decade will be a natural accompaniment to an emerging post-industrial society, the more urgent and dramatic problems are likely to be those of a super-industrial society.[13] The term "super-industrial" refers mainly to the high rate of innovation in a modern economy and to the degree to which projects are frequently undertaken on such a large scale that various unintended side effects — externalities, as economists call them — are sometimes of greater consequence than the intended effects. These issues can pose serious problems for modern societies.

In particular, a super-industrial economy poses major problems in three ways: (1) it confronts societies with many new technologies, some of which cannot be fully or even adequately controlled; (2) many problems are of an unprecedented nature; and (3) since some of these problems may grow exponentially (at least for a while), societies may not become aware of them until they have already become critical. For example, super-industrial growth could conceivably bring with it such problems as:

- an ecological catastrophe from large scale interference with the biosphere;

- a genetic calamity from thousands of new chemicals coming on to the market each year, about whose long term effects we know practically nothing;

- worldwide epidemics or "pandemics", owing to increased travel;

- the large scale appearance of drug-resistant pests and viruses due to an excessive use of drugs and antibiotics;

- the danger of an Armageddon, as an increasing number of smaller countries come to possess nuclear, thermonuclear, or biological weapons.

Indeed, there is no way that a super-industrial economy can exist without endangering the environment and the general quality of life to some degree. Various examples from the recent past illustrate this point: defective bolts in DC-10 aircraft, various oil blowouts that pollute parts of the sea and beaches, PCB in the food chain, and, in an example that is certainly familiar to Australians, the fall of Skylab. In the future, the ozone layer might be depleted; a new ice age might be caused by an excessive burning of fossil fuels; or lakes and streams might turn to acid as a result of insufficient health and safety standards.

However, new technologies can solve problems as well as cause them. Indeed, it is often said that technology by itself is neither beneficial nor harmful: this is correct if one thinks of technology as a whole, if one believes there are no intrinsic tendencies in technology. We prefer not to take such a strong position, and to recognize that some technologies are more likely to be harmful than beneficial. Intrinsic to the concept of technological progress is the possibility that it may get out of control.

Whether technology will benefit or harm society depends mainly on how it is used and what one's values are. In terms of most people's values, the majority of our technological problems can be cured by a relatively small amount of self-restraint and a large amount of new technology. Take, for example, the problem of the automobile. It is easy to imagine that by self-restraint one could cut pollution by a factor of two. One could even more easily imagine that through new technology one could within a decade or two cut pollution by a factor of twenty to one hundred. This projection will make no impression on those who are hostile to the motor vehicle simply because it is a symbol of everything that they dislike about modern societies. But for those who basically like the automobile and wish to alleviate its costs, this projection is impressive. Indeed, for the first group, some of the other harm which they claim is caused by the automobile — such as accidents, suburban sprawl, the break up of family life — will actually be aggravated by the car's being made more acceptable because it is less polluting. Thus, the key to whether any particular technology will benefit rather than harm society lies not only in how it is used but also in the value systems and criteria for deciding how it is used.

As industrialization spreads to more and more countries, and the world economy as a whole becomes super-industrial, a "problem-prone super-industrial economy" may emerge, in which the externalities tend to be new, unclear, and difficult to control. When and if these external effects can be satisfactorily understood and controlled (or at least alleviated), this super-industrial economy becomes "problem-controlled" rather than "problem-prone". But this would only occur if individuals, groups, and societies as a whole sought to deal with the difficulties.

Enough problems of a super-industrial nature have already arisen to necessitate a redefinition of the very process of economic decision-making. New perceptions of what is rational and acceptable have greatly affected business decisions, government policies, and political processes in all advanced capitalist nations.

For example, the appearance of new priorities — and to some degree new value systems — has changed the manner in which public utilities operate, and led to much tighter regulations over the automobile industry. These new priorities have doubtless lowered the aggregate volume of investment by raising the required rate of return on projects involving high pollution-control expenditures. Moreover, throughout the ACNs, so-called public interest groups have increasingly sought a voice in technological decisions, such as the siting of nuclear power plants and the construction of super-highways. The most familiar case of this kind in Australia is the controversy over the export of uranium.

Social Limits to Economic Growth

A decade ago, the traditional Western concept of progress was a firmly held proposition. This was true not only in the West, but throughout much of the rest of the world as well, certainly among Western-influenced elites in non-Western countries. Yet by the early 1970s, a completely different viewpoint had become influential, and often dominant, particularly in the ACNs. This new view held that the world was running out of resources, that pollution was nearly out of control, and that management itself was becoming impossibly difficult. Hence, it was said, the future would probably not be as good as the past.

The best illustration of this change may be seen in the enormous popularity of the Club of Rome's report, *The Limits to Growth*,[14] one of the most influential books of the 1970s. Its basic premise is so simple as to seem almost self-evident: the world's finite resources must eventually be depleted; the only question is how soon this will happen. The model assumed that a finite supply of material would be confronting an exponentially growing demand. Growth was assumed to continue roughly at current rates until it would run into disastrous physical constraints. If one accepts the basic premise, then the dangers posed by continuing growth are extremely grave: however big the pie, it is being eaten away. Without going through the argument in detail here, we reject the fixed pie metaphor. It is much more accurate to think of

Growth Rate (Percentage)

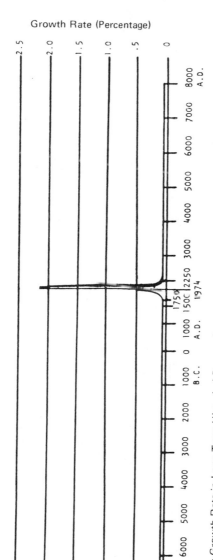

Fig. 2.3 Population Growth Rate in Long-Term Historical Perspective
Source: Ronald Freeman and Bernard Berelson, "The Human Population", *Scientific American*, September 1974, p. 36—37.

the supply of resources as a process or system for creating and exploiting various assets, and using them in many different ways. The world has continually found, not only more resources, but new kinds of resources and new ways to extract and use both the old and new resources, as well as newly developed substitutes for many traditional substitutes.

What about the widely-held assumption that population is growing at a rate that is itself growing? Figure 2.3 shows the rate of growth of world population in the perspective of a sixteen thousand year time frame; the resulting "spike" suggests that the Great Transition stands out as a unique period in world history. The graph shown here first appeared in *Scientific American* in 1974, and later versions have been regularly referred to in leading newspapers and magazines since then. Nonetheless, few people seem aware that total population growth is not an indefinite exponential but rather an S-shaped, or logistic, curve in which first the rate of growth and subsequently total growth tapers off. The peak in the spike, that is, the peak in the growth rate of world population, is now widely estimated by demographers to have occurred in the early 1960s — more than fifteen years ago. Indeed, each revision of population data provided by the United Nations in recent years has pushed the estimated peak in the rate of growth of world population further back in time, and projected growth rates have been successively lowered. In our view, the now demonstrable fact that percentage population growth rates have peaked and are now declining requires a profound change in one's perspective on the future.

To be sure, this peak in the percentage rate of growth of world population masks some distinctly dissimilar trends among regions and countries (see Figure 2.4). Although birth rates have been declining in developed countries since at least the 1950s, absolute additions to population will continue to be high in some regions of the world even after the world growth rate has peaked. From an estimated world population of slightly over 4 billion in 1975, United Nations estimates project about 6.2 billion persons in the year 2000, a 50 per cent increase in twenty-five years. By the second half of the twenty-first century, there are likely to be between 10 and 12 billion individuals on earth.

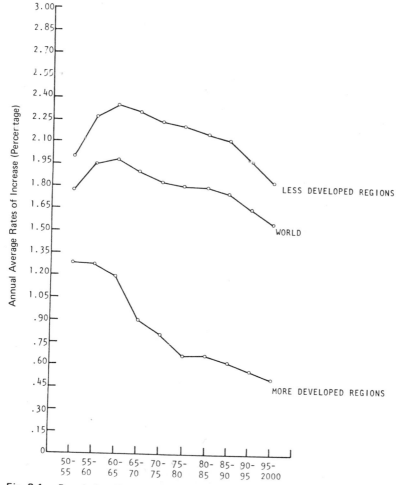

Fig. 2.4 Population Growth Trends in the World, More Developed and Less Developed Regions, 1950–2000

Source: United Nations, *World Population Trends and Prospects by Country, 1950–2000, Summary Report of the 1978 Assessment* (New York, ST/ESA/ SER, R/33, 1979) Various Pages.

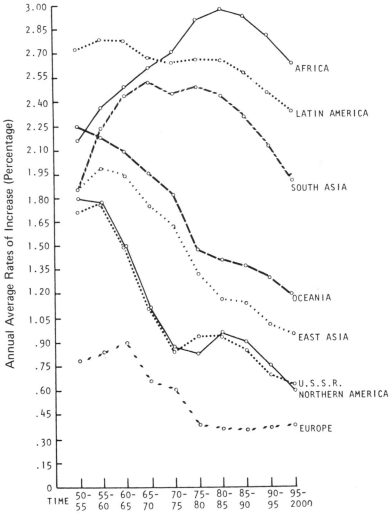

Fig. 2.5 Population Growth Trends in Eight Major Areas of World, 1950–2000
Source: United Nations, *World Population Trends and Prospects by Country, 1950–2000, Summary Report of the 1978 Assessment* (New York, ST/ESA/SER. R/33, 1979) Various Pages.

Moreover, sharp population pressures will continue in selected developing countries. (Figure 2.5 gives a breakdown of the most recent UN estimates for population projections by region.) In those countries where rates of population growth will still be high, correspondingly high rates of investment and economic growth will be needed to maintain per capita income levels. Their labour forces will increase more rapidly than population, which will tend to depress wages. Even if the world as a whole faces few resource shortages, rapid population growth in some regions or countries may lead to selective supply shortages or even to confrontations between resources and demand. On the other hand, slower population growth in the developed countries may be associated with slower labour force growth, contributing in turn to slower economic growth (although perhaps not slower per capita growth) and slower import demand growth. In this context, migration issues will become increasingly important; the main cause of population growth in the developed countries will change from natural increase to immigration. As a result, migration will become a more important foreign policy issue.

These population trends will have important long-term effects on the world economy. Yet they are so little known among seemingly educated non-specialists that one is forced to ask why. The explanation lies in a profound change in value systems in affluent countries.

Economic growth, like population growth, is a relatively recent phenomenon: it was first achieved by Western culture only two centuries ago. For the previous ten millenia, no civilization had achieved the kind of sustained economic progress that is literally taken for granted today. Ancient China, Greece, Rome, and India all had technology of a relatively high order — at least in their day. Their failure to attain sustained economic progress stemmed less from a lack of technology than from societal or cultural attitudes that constituted social limits to economic growth. In particular, these ancient societies rejected the concept of creative destruction. Thus rapid growth was not permitted if it would have led to destruction of the old in order to make way for the new — or to a change in the balance of power.

Surprisingly perhaps, many attitudes that have emerged in the

ACNs in recent years could bring to a close the kind of sustained economic growth these affluent countries have been enjoying since the Industrial Revolution. If their growth were to stop or slow drastically, the main cause would probably be a re-emergence of various social limits to growth.

These newly emerging values seem likely to play an increasingly important role in the politics, culture, and daily life of all affluent countries. They are listed in Table 2.1 as "Some New Emphases". Their most telling impact is on the prospects for economic growth in the advanced capitalist nations. Indeed, it is difficult to think of any intellectual change in the ACNs in the second half of the twentieth century that has had — or seems likely to have — greater consequences for economic growth.

The widespread disappearance — albeit mostly among intellectuals — of faith in progress has spawned an entire literature of pessimism during the last decade. Such titles as *The Coming Dark Age*,[15] *The End of the American Future*[16] and *Where the Wasteland Ends*[17] are typical examples. Charles Birch, a biologist at the University of Sydney, takes roughly the same approach in a widely read analysis aimed at an Australian audience.[18] These works reflect a startling loss of confidence in the traditional premises of economic progress: the value of economic growth and prosperity, the use of rational thought to control man's environment, and acceptance of material advancement as a sign of intellectual and moral growth. As a result, a corresponding shift has occurred towards public policies that distort market forces for non-market purposes, and generally interfere with social patterns. All this reflects a poor understanding of how economic and technological processes have worked in the past — and even more of how they work today.

A contributing factor behind this trend is a phenomenon we refer to as "educated incapacity". This is the tendency, most pronounced in the public sector but widespread in business as well, for top-level decisions increasingly to be made by highly educated persons without direct experience in, or serious knowledge of, the processes they administer. The phrase "educated incapacity" is a modification of the idea of "trained incapacity", which the economist Thorstein Veblen used to refer, among other things, to the inability of those with engineering or sociology training to understand certain things they would have been able to understand if they had not had this training.[19] Indeed, because top-level people are so well-educated and self-confident, they typically cannot imagine the degree to which they are out of touch with the specific issues confronting them. To be sure, it is important from their own viewpoint and from that of society that they pick up advanced knowledge in certain fields, but their doing so usually has the consequence of narrowing their perspective. Hence, they are less able to deal with issues unrelated to their field of specialization.

This tendency is most evident among a certain sector of the upper middle class, described as the "New Class" by Irving Kristol, B. Bruce-Briggs, Daniel Bell, Daniel Patrick Moynihan, and others, including ourselves.[20] The New Class is a sociological, not a political, category: in fact, the political persuasions of New Class members are spread over a wide range. As a part of a broader group of people who can be characterized as upper middle class, members of the New Class in the U.S. are likely to have family incomes between $25,000 and $100,000 per year, to have attended university, and to be engaged in white collar occupations. For example, a large part of academia, the media, and most so-called "public interest" groups belong to the New Class. Often this kind of work is associated with a lack of practical experience that can all too easily convert even the most well intentioned goals into extremely counter-productive policies.

Typically, members of the New Class deny that they exert themselves on behalf of their own class interests. They feel, often unconsciously, that since they are the most intelligent or best educated part of the population, they should naturally set the standard for others. The New Class sees itself as a "progressive" force, overturning the "oppressive" dominance of "selfish" profit-oriented business values, "dehumanizing" organizations, "blind" technology, "crass" materialism, and "commercialized" vulgarity that its members see all around them. (These same phenomena, incidentally, are seen as liberating, useful, enjoyable, or admirable by virtually any lower middle class person who seeks to improve his or her position over the course of a lifetime.)

Table 2.1 Some New Emphases

MOSTLY REGULATION–TYPE ISSUES

THE NEW EMPHASIS	It is both **NATURAL AND INEVITABLE** that increasing affluence and the increasing capabilities of advanced technology make it easier to:	But the new emphases can cause **CREEPING STAGNATION** and other problems, when they go too far:
1. Selective Risk Avoidance	Reduce most risks and choose more freely and flexibly which risks will be run. (It will still be necessary, however, to run some risks.)	Innovators, entrepreneurs, businessmen, and "Do-ers" are forced to bear all the risks and the burden of proof as if only they, and not society as a whole, benefited from their efforts.
2. Localism	Put more emphasis on protecting the stability of local neighbourhoods and communities. However, there can still be disturbances and annoyances as a result of many normal developments or high priority projects (whether locally or externally generated).	Virtually all disturbances of local interests are blocked despite the larger needs of society; policies clearly favour the "ins" over the "outs" for example, local vested interests over new or outside interests).
3. Protection of Environment and Ecology	Repair some of the past damage and be able to afford both protection and improvement of existing environment and ecology. In addition, the magnitude and complexity of a modern economy raise many justifiable concerns about the possibility of irrevocable damage or major catastrophes. Many more remote and implausible concerns can also be taken more seriously (for example, ozone layer or climate change).	Pursuit of environmental and ecological protection without regard to economic cost, or to other social goals; emotional, politically motivated, and demagogic discussions of risks from new and old projects. Attempts to create a risk-free world or to replace faustian man and western religious concepts with passive man and "oriental" subservience to nature and often a "spiritual" disregard of materialistic objectives.

NEW CONCEPTS ABOUT ACCEPTABLE BEHAVIOUR & ACTIVITIES

(NEW EMPHASIS)	(NATURAL & INEVITABLE VERSION)	(CREEPING STAGNATION VERSION)
4. Comfort, Safety, Leisure and Health Regulations	Satisfy basic survival needs rather easily. Indeed since these can almost (but never completely) be taken for granted, there is then greater interest in (and ability to afford) more emphasis on the next level of need; these desiderata are on that next level.	Given excessive priorities and/or mandated by government in rigid and unrealistic regulations approaching "health and safety authoritarianism". A general disregard or under-emphasis of cost/effectiveness criteria.
5. Happiness and Hedonism	Emphasize personal enjoyment and less inhibited gratification of various desires. De-emphasize success, achievement, self-discipline, conscience, rigid puritanical standards, etc., as the sole basis for a satisfactory lifestyle.	Becoming the major explicit goals in life, to be sought directly rather than indirectly (that is as a by-product of other goals). Nothing except human life, here and now, is of greater priority.
6. Public Welfare and Social Justice	Be more concerned about equity; in particular, the goal that individuals, groups, and regions should not be "unduly" harmed or left out of society's prosperity. Welfare for the deserving poor and many of the handicapped becomes a right rather than a privilege.	Life must be made "fair". Equality of result, not equality of opportunity. Justice should not be blind. Historical inequities should be compensated for, as well as rectified. Welfare for all who need it (or even want it) as a right rather than a privilege
7. Growing Pluralism and Freedom in the Larger and Higher Societal Objectives	Provide increased education, physical well-being and security for all, and reduce the pressures due to once overriding external imperatives; nor need there be so many pressures toward a conforming society. All this also allows for, or even encourages, growth of interest and social groups with a wide variety of objectives and images of the future, and more pluralism and freedom in life styles as well as in the arts and literature.	A naive, emotional, and rigid over-rejection of past attitudes and values; this can lead to a loss of nerve, will, optimism, confidence, and morale regarding economic progress and technological advancement; and encourage excessive tendencies toward radical chic, trendy trends, and disastrous erosion of past social standards and structures. Elitist attitudes and indifference or hostility toward the aspirations and values of the silent majority. Finally an emphasis on the adversary culture in life styles and the values of the arts and literature.

Table 2.1 cont.

| | RE—EVALUATION OF BASIC SOCIETAL PRIORITIES | |
(NEW EMPHASIS)	(NATURAL & INEVITABLE VERSION)	(CREEPING STAGNATION VERSION)
8. Progress Less Central	Reduce public interest in technology, economic progress, and big projects; also, an erosion of the work ethic and many other traditional middle class attitudes and mores.	General anti-technology, anti-economic development, anti-middle class attitudes (for example, "small is better" and "limits to growth" movements). Also, enormous resources can be allocated or great economic costs accepted to promote emphases 1–7 above.
9. Less Faith in Market Forces (Adam Smith's "Invisible Hand") and Utilitarian and Rational Ideologies	Place less emphasis on market forces, individual entrepreneurship, and "rugged individualism". A weakened belief that the results of these forces will be largely beneficial to the society as a whole, even when they are successful from the viewpoint of the individual.	Increasing interest in social control and overall planning of the economy (but mostly with "new class" values and attitudes and by "input-output" theorists). New emphasis on social responsibility and explicit representation of the "public interest" in running corporations. A movement toward socialism.
10. Growing Indifference to Business and Economic Motivation, Morale, and Efficiency	Show more concern for other social and cultural goals. After all, the richer and more technological the society, the greater is the likelihood that more riches and more technology will bring diminishing marginal returns.	Regulatory attitudes that are opposed to or just indifferent to the welfare of business. "Big business" becomes the arch-villain of many organized movements and much popular literature. The availability of acceptable jobs is assumed to be a right rather than a reward for effort and achievement. The productivity and profitability of business are taken for granted or considered irrelevant (or even reprehensible).

RE—EVALUATION OF PERSONAL & FAMILY PRIORITIES

(NEW EMPHASIS)	(NATURAL & INEVITABLE VERSION)	(CREEPING STAGNATION VERSION)
11. Modern Family and Social Values	De-emphasize many of the thirteen traditional levers (values) such as work orientation, being a man or woman, religion, patriotism and other "square" values, and place more emphasis on aesthetic, cultural, and personal (human) values.	Emphasis by the educational system and family on happiness, adjustment, and self-fulfilment; almost total de-emphasis of objective achievement, responsible behaviour, scholarship, good citizenship, patriotism, and job-oriented skills and attitudes.
12. Concern With Self	Take continued well-being of society, community, and family largely for granted; opportunities for personal development and self-expression expand.	An almost anarchic and/or narcissistic self indulgence. "Meism" is often accompanied by a cultist or fashionable emphasis on fulfilling one-self as an independent human being (for example, self-engendering).
13. New Rites, Ceremonies, and celebrations — New Sources of Meaning, Purpose, and Prestige	Regard survival and economic development values as less important. New behaviour emerges both against and instead of tradition. New values, institutions, and goals provide new standards of evaluation, comparison, and status. Culture and society evolve and change.	Protest as a way of life, as moral fulfilment, and as a mode of socializing and entertainment (particularly for the young adult). A revival of paganism, superstition, and gnostic rites and religions. "Negative success" status from impeding growth and progress; the dropout hero; manic "small is beautiful" and back to nature ideologies and fancies. To "rebel without a cause" becomes heroic.

Note: These "new" emphases are not, of course, completely new. However, they are becoming relatively pervasive in every developed country, but especially in the atlantic protestant culture area (that is, Scandinavia, Holland, England, United States, Canada, and perhaps Australia and New Zealand). These new emphases are held with special intensity by the neo-liberal and humanist-left members of what is sometimes called the new class, which we often call the symbolist class — a class defined by the characteristic that it makes its living by understanding, interpreting, creating, and using symbols — that is, by expertise in analytic, literary, artistic, educational, religious, and aesthetic activities.

It is probably true that, on balance, the members of the New Class become relatively worse off as economic growth proceeds.[21] But the New Class is wrong when it asserts that society *as a whole* will suffer from further economic growth. Indeed, most writings on the pros and cons of growth almost completely ignore the otherwise obvious tendency of their New Class authors to confuse their own class interests and values with those of society as a whole. This confusion of interests contributes to the extreme positions taken by members of the New Class against economic growth and other manifestations of progress, as that term is normally understood.

Structural Change and Adjustment

The economies of the advanced capitalist nations changed considerably during the past decade. Some changes continued or accelerated earlier long-term trends; others seemed to reflect sudden or apparent discontinuities. As a result, the decade ahead will see more extensive structural change in the ACNs than during the 1950s and 1960s. Among the more important of these changes are the following:

1. A seemingly permanent slowing in the long-term growth rate of productivity and per capita output;
2. An increased growth in international trade, relative to output;
3. Relatively high (but probably declining) inflation rates;
4. A shift in the composition of employment and output from manufacturing to services;
5. A changed social and political context, including increased public demands on government budgets, a seemingly increased inability to respond to these demands, and an increased need to deal simultaneously with domestic and international considerations;
6. A dramatic increase in the importance of middle-income countries as a source of worldwide growth.

Despite the need for rapid adjustment to these trends, in practice the ACNs have experienced a slowdown in the rate at which they can make adjustments. Therefore, the length of the adjustment period will be substantial, and will doubtless vary from country to country.

In the mid-1970s, the combination of slower growth in the long-term sense and cyclical decline in the short- to medium-term sense produced serious problems of overcapacity throughout the industrial world, though, again, the degree varied from country to country.[27] By 1979, a combination of adjustments — notably some degree of cyclical recovery and some retirement of excess capacity — brought most industries in most of the ACNs back nearly to full capacity. However, these adjustments failed to trigger the kind of self-generating growth characteristic of previous periods.

At the same time, the ACNs continue to face the prospect that sources of previous growth will weaken. These declines reflect, among other things: (1) the end of any catch-up from the Great Depression and World War II; (2) the completion of many subsequent infrastructure projects; (3) declining population growth; (4) a relative decline in military spending; (5) distortions to long-term planning caused by steadily rising inflation; (6) an increased number of non-tariff trade barriers; (7) the topping out of demand for such previously leading sectors as automobiles and consumer durables; (8) the inability of governments to increase demand while inflation rates are high; and (9) the growth of the New Emphases.

Despite generally higher labour force participation rates and a more favourable ratio of working age to total population, the total labour force in the ACNs will grow less quickly in the years ahead than in the recent past; also, despite an increased education level and a more experienced work force, the productivity added by these gains will probably be less than in the recent past. On average, rates of capital investment in the ACNs will probably remain sluggish, though perhaps less so than in the 1970s. Rates of technological advance may slow as well, although the evidence here is more ambiguous; in any case, the ACNs seem to be facing declining opportunities for technological catch-up, probable declines in the rate of return on investment in research and development, and an increasing diversion of research and development toward meeting environmental, health, and safety standards.

There are, however, important countervailing trends — the most important being the likelihood that long-term cyclical forces will still play their historical role, though perhaps only slowly, and return the system to a more expansionist phase, roughly along the lines of the archetype long cycle. Among other things, new technologies, new potential growth sectors, a continuing reaction against excessive government regulation throughout the ACNs, and the continued expansion of the middle-income countries all suggest that the slowdown in world economic growth since 1974 may be bottoming out. If so, average world growth rates should be on the rise again by the mid-to-late 1980s. Growth rates for the ACNs over the next decade are likely to be lower than during the first postwar generation, though probably higher than those experienced since 1973. Growth rates for the middle-income countries should follow a similar pattern, except that their increase in dynamism is likely to be greater than the ACNs. As adjustment proceeds, growth should strengthen in both groups.

As the middle-income countries become more developed, they will sell more goods to the ACNs, but they will also buy more. Indeed, a major reason the middle-income countries try so hard to increase their exports is to earn the foreign exchange needed to increase their imports. Both exports and imports are required if they are to grow. Trade problems between the developed and developing countries arise not from the basic process of "creative destruction", which is *on balance* beneficial for all parties that take part in it, but from the fact that those who are hurt become more activist than those who benefit. The disturbances and pain incurred by trading partners may be felt more than the benefits to them of increased sales. In general, the middle-income countries will gradually move from a comparative advantage in such things as textiles, basic steel, and mass market consumer electronics to something resembling that of the ACNs today. (See Table 2.2.) At the same time, the ACNs should be moving toward increasingly specialized industries and services involving advanced technology and the application of their previous experience. Indeed, the ACNs may find themselves increasingly challenged in the years ahead, but, unless they turn against growth altogether, they should also find themselves productive

Rich	Middle-Income	Poor
(Advanced Capitalist Nations and, to a lesser extent, Communist Europe)	(especially the new industrial countries – South Korea, Taiwan, Brazil, Mexico, Portugal, Spain, Greece, Turkey, Yugoslavia, Hong Kong, Singapore)	1. Tourism, second homes, retirement homes
1. Services – human and organizational	1. Mass market quality consumer electronics	2. Exported labour
2. Investment		3. Cheap consumer electronics
3. Other knowledge and knowledge related industries	2. Conventional ships (including super large ships)	4. Cheap shoes and clothes
4. Advanced technology	3. Ordinary steel, other basic metals	5. Cheap bicycles and toys
5. Advanced agriculture	4. Motor vehicle parts (very soon, motor vehicles)	6. Many commodities
6. Some raw materials		7. Many spare parts
7. Specialized, proprietary, and/or esoteric or fashionable consumer goods	5. Some petrochemicals	8. Cheap sporting goods
	6. Medium priced textiles (natural and synthetic)	9. Souvenirs and bric-a-brac
8. Some heavy industry, petrochemicals, and specialty steel	7. Many machine tools, expensive but conventional tool and die components, etc.	10. Other national resources
		11. Some rip-offs
9. Large construction jobs, oil exploration, prospecting, computerized analysis of above, etc.	8. Simple motors, engines, generators	12. Esoteric activities (e.g., importation of archeologists, Peace Corps, missionaries, international officials and commissions, development experts, etc.)
10. Pop and mass culture and entertainment.	9. Medium quality bicycles, toys, golf-carts, motor scooters, and motorcycles	13. A gradual (sometimes rapid) movement into the arena now being exploited by the middle income countries.
	10. Low-priced shoes, ordinary mass-produced clothes	
	11. Typewriters, simple office machines, some modern small calculators	
	12. Sewing machines, chinaware, silver, cookware, many other household appliances	
	13. Ordinary and some precision optical equipment, some quality cameras (under licence)	
	14. Rip-offs: patent and copyright infringements, cheap copies of popular goods, etc.	
	15. Almost all of the items on the poor countries list.	

and competitive in many new areas. But they must accept that, for continued growth, such adjustments are necessary, if to some degree costly in the short term.

Attempts by the ACNs to preserve the status quo might temporarily bring the pleasures and relaxations of a relatively static state, but eventually these attemps would be likely to fail. The middle-income countries of the world — particularly those in the Asia-Pacific region — almost certainly have enough drive and ambition to maintain higher-than-average growth rates, even in an environment of increased protectionism. In such an environment, the growth process would be more difficult and of course take longer. But by seeking high growth, these countries create conditions that the ACNs must face up to in any event. In a more positive sense, the high growth rates of the middle-income countries help pull up the growth rate of the rich countries, or at least help keep them from falling further. Even if people in the ACNs eventually decide to slow their growth, the slowing down that is already occurring is premature. The ACNs would do much better to restructure their economies so as to be able to take advantage of the next stage in world growth, a stage that will probably be led by the middle-income countries. By riding this wave, the ACNs would make it even bigger, and more durable.

Some years hence, perhaps shortly after the turn of the century, the ACNs might justifiably begin to coast even more in response to social limits to growth than they do now, but this would occur only after the middle-income countries had become much richer, and the ACNs a bit richer as well. Even then, this same question of how hard to work versus how much to coast — how much to invest versus how much to consume — would still have to be faced. More than 20 per cent of the world, at that point, would still be as poor as it was by historical standards, that is U.S. $300 GNP per capita or less. But once today's middle-income countries achieve higher standards of living, this trade-off between growth and stability would not have to be faced as starkly as it should be faced today. A shift toward so-called stable growth rates by both the rich and the future newly rich countries would then be more justifiable than it is today.

Some Particular Problems Facing Australia

In discussing the future of Australia, it is useful to have a theoretical understanding of some particular problems facing the country as a result of its natural resource endowments or certain trends in modern economies that have proved particularly intractable.

Comparative Advantage and Natural Resources

Australia has traditionally earned a large proportion of its exports from the rural sector. In the early- to mid-nineteenth century, wool was overwhelmingly *the* export commodity. Since the mining boom of the 1950s and 1960s, mineral resources, particularly iron ore and coal, have been added to wool, wheat, and meat to the point where the agriculture and mining sectors together now make up roughly 75 per cent of the country's exports in terms of value. Although the endowments in terms of land and resources that make these exports possible are enviable assets in almost every respect, they do make it at least relatively more difficult to maintain a competitive manufacturing sector.

This problem has been widely discussed among Australian economists in the wake of two articles by Robert Gregory in 1976.[23] These emphasized the point that a sharp increase in exports of natural resources drives up the foreign exchange value of a currency, and that wages throughout the society tend to be driven up if there is one highly productive sector, such as mineral development, that has high wages. As many of Gregory's economist colleagues pointed out, neither of these effects is necessarily applicable only to exports of natural resources or to differentially high wages in the natural resources sector. But these effects are certainly more visible if they stem from an easily identifiable cause such as the mining sector. This problem is discussed in terms of a simple model.

Assume first that the world is comprised of a number of countries roughly equal in size to Australia, and all with about the same population, value systems, and level of development, but with one significant difference: Australia has a much larger

potential for producing resources and commodities than other
countries. Also assume that Australians have failed to take
advantage of this great potential. Under these circumstances, all
the countries in the group trade among one another and minor
differences make for comparative advantages in one or another
sector. All these countries then have roughly similar economic
structures in terms of the percentage of the population engaged in
the agriculture and mining, manufacturing, and service sectors.

Now assume that Australia's commodity and resource potential is developed: the productivity of the primary sector goes up
enormously. Some of this increased productivity is accounted for
by an increase in the wages of individuals employed in the primary sector and some by increased earnings to companies and
investors in that sector. Surplus resources and commodities are
exported to the rest of the world because Australia now has a
huge comparative advantage in these fields and much more production than it can use itself. To pay for those Australian commodities and resources, other countries need Australian dollars.
Hence, there is a strong demand for Australia's currency, and the
price of Australian dollars is driven upwards. In addition, Australians who are working in the manufacturing and service sectors
want to earn at least as much as people working in the agriculture
and mining sector. At this point, of course, people will start moving from the manufacturing and service sector into the
agriculture and mining sector. There is a tendency then for the
wages of the manufacturing and service sector to go up and for
those in the agricultural and mining sector to go down. A new
balance will be reached at an intermediate point between the two
original numbers. At the same time, the country can afford to
export less to buy the same amount of imports. The result is — or
should be — that everyone in Australia lives better because
imports are cheaper and salaries have gone up across the board.

However, as these adjustments take place, imported manufactured goods now have a great advantage over locally manufactured goods. There is then a strong tendency for Australian
manufacturers, under the twin pressures of increased domestic
costs and decreased foreign prices, simply to go out of business,
or at least to become rapidly uncompetitive. Hence the manufac-

turing sector will either shrink or need protection. The degree of protection it gets is also inclined to be abused, which tends in turn to make the manufacturing sector even less efficient.

In principle, the above sequence of events need not occur. Australians might use their increased income from the production of commodities and resources to make themselves more competitive through the use of increased capital built up by the development of resources. The more productive the resource industries are, the more pressure there will be on the manufacturing industry, but if there is enough increased capital to finance increases in productivity, it is still possible to operate a competitive manufacturing sector. For many industries, of course, such improved productivity will simply be impossible. This is particularly likely for low value-added industries, and relatively less technological industries. Thus, for a country like Australia, any comparative advantage in manufacturing has to be found in industries in which other countries would have difficulty introducing a comparable degree of capital, technology, and training through which Australia can increase the value added content of its manufactured goods. Australian manufacturers might also seek to organize vertically integrated production systems, placing the lower value-added segments of production offshore, in nearby developing countries, and limiting domestic production to higher value-added stages of the total process. This is more easily said than done, of course.

It is equally important to note that the extra income from increased exports can be used in many ways that need not increase the exchange rate. For example, it can be: (1) invested overseas; (2) invested domestically to increase the productivity and efficiency of other domestic industries; (3) used to pay back foreign investors in Australia, or (4) used to accumulate foreign exchange reserves. If tax and other incentives were consciously designed to take advantage of the earnings from Australia's commodity and mineral production, the country would have a much greater likelihood of operating a large manufacturing sector alongside an efficient agriculture and mining sector.

Inflation and Indexation

The effects of inflation can be very different depending on the degree to which they are anticipated, on the accuracy with which the rate of inflation can be predicted, and on the degree to which indexation can be kept within bounds. In any case, both the inflation itself and the anticipation of inflation have important effects in distorting the smooth operations of an economic system. While the effects can be varied in the short term, any sustained inflation is likely to make the whole system less efficient in the long term.

This section discusses certain effects of indexation, which seem either to have been overlooked or to have had a particularly strong effect on the Australian economy because of the ease with which the decisions of the Arbitration Commission have enabled wage increases to be passed from one sector of the economy to another. The term "indexation", as used here, refers both to *de jure* and *ad hoc* compensation for inflation-based price increases. In actual effect, it makes little difference whether adjustments to a higher price level occur rapidly because of *ad hoc* actions that are taken immediately after an increase in the index, or because of a formal, legal connection between the adjustment and the index.

Using another simple model, assume that a fraction M of an economy is indexed. Assume also that some kind of a shock depresses the living standards of almost everybody — for example, an increase in the price of oil charged by an outside supplier. If there were no indexation, everybody would find that oil, and products in which oil is used, went up in price. Under these circumstances, people who bought oil or products of oil would find themselves living less well. Moreover, because more money is used to buy oil, there is less money to buy other things and the whole economy suffers, though the overall price level remains constant.

Then, assume that the central bank allows for an increase in the money supply so that there is no pressure on the non-energy part of the economy, but because of the increase in energy prices the cost of living index rises. If a fraction M of the economy is indexed, then the extent to which the higher price of oil increases the value of the index is fully compensated for in the M portion of the overall economy. Real incomes in this sector are maintained despite the increase in the price of oil. This occurs because the indexing system does not distinguish between a truly inflationary effect, stemming from purely monetary phenomena (that is, a change in the measuring instrument), and a real change in world conditions. As a result, the need for adjusting to such real world conditions is shifted completely away from the indexed M fraction of the economy to that fraction (1-M) of the economy that is not indexed. As a result, the unindexed part of the economy has to bear the complete cost of the adjustment. The price of goods and services in the unindexed part of the economy goes up while the indexed part of the economy is completely protected from the problem. This is unfair, of course, and creates enormous strains. Finally, even within the indexed part of the economy, since different groups buy different market baskets, some gain more than others.

In the past, many economists have felt that a steady inflation was no more than a purely monetary phenomenon that did not really disturb the "natural order of things", and was therefore tolerable as long as it was steady, predictable, and corrected for. We would argue, however, that the effects of indexing can make the economy and the price level extremely vulnerable to outside shocks, as well as shifting the burden of bearing outside shocks (and of making adjustments) from, more or less, the entire economy to that part of the economy that has not been indexed. The longer the inflation continues, the more likely it is that a higher percentage of the economy will be indexed, either through formal, legal arrangements or through *ad hoc* pressures generated because of the greater sensitivity and militancy of various groups. This in turn means that, the longer the inflation lasts, the more the economy may become prone to an explosive inflation. Since the effects of inflation are rarely homogeneous, these effects differ in various parts of the economy. Hence, even if the effects are corrected for, on average, they will still have serious effects on many specific individuals, groups, industries, and products.

Unemployment and Recession

Many Australians argue that unemployment and recession are the most important issues facing the country at the moment. Many also believe that, even if fighting unemployment and recession would lead to greater inflation, public opinion would prefer to put up with additional inflation. This has simply not been true in many countries in the 1970s. The average person has become much more upset by inflation than by the prospect of unemployment and recession. As a result of the Great Depression, people who have not faced the rigours of inflation as much as they have faced (or studied) the difficulties stemming from the Depression do not realize how strongly opinions have changed in recent years. Thus, what might be called the traditional sensitivity toward unemployment and recession prevails among leading economists and politicians, even though, as inflation rates have risen in the 1970s, the general public in the ACNs has become increasingly concerned about losses due to inflation. Both problems are important, but politicians would do well to recognize, not only the economic ill effects of inflation, but also the shift in public opinion that makes it more likely nowadays to lose elections because of excessive inflation than excessive unemployment.

Certainly unemployment can have catastrophic effects on the individual and the family, but these ill effects are now much alleviated. This is not to say that they never occur, or to argue that one should be callous when they do occur. Still, one of the main reasons for unemployment today stems from the very success achieved by an affluent capitalist economy. Partly because of minimum wage laws, partly because of unemployment insurance and other social welfare expenditures, and partly because of the general level of affluence, most people in ACNs no longer take jobs they feel are inappropriate to their status or station; nor will they drop their salary requirements to "ridiculously" low levels.[24] This is an important cause of youth unemployment, for example.

In any case, it seems quite likely that, for the next decade or so, almost every ACN is going to have higher levels of unemployment than during *La Deuxième Belle Epoque*. This is not to say that governments should ignore problems of unemployment, but rather that these programs should be more in the style of a rifle shot than a shotgun blast. In particular, massive manipulation of aggregate demand by monetary and fiscal policies is simply not going to work well, largely because of the extraordinarily inflation-prone nature of advanced capitalist economies. Indeed, by exacerbating inflation in situations where stagflation is already the main problem, such policies actually exacerbate unemployment as well.

Many of these points about unemployment apply to recessions as well. Moderately frequent, weak recessions should be thought of as a normal part of the operation of a dynamic capitalist system, and a major objective of economic policy should be less to defer recessions than to try to make them short and shallow. It is important — perhaps essential — for the successful operation of a capitalist economy to have both perceived and real "downside risks". A recession is simply one concrete expression of such down-side risks. As such, it can be a healthy, as well as an inevitable, part of a growing and dynamic capitalist economy.

If a recession can allow for or force through needed adjustments and reimpose financial and labour discipline, then the GNP "lost" because the economy was operating below capacity could — and should — be viewed as an acceptable price for maintaining a healthy competitive system. It is not waste, but upkeep. Recessions can not only be useful, but under modern conditions they are much less painful than they used to be — particularly if they are short and mild. In this sense, modern economies are similar to land areas prone to earthquakes. Relatively moderate tremors relieve geological strains and decrease the chance for a really big earthquake. Furthermore, they remind residents of the problem, encourage them to build better structures, and damage rather than demolish weak ones. Painful as the moderate tremors are, they are not as painful as total destruction. If such moderate earthquakes do not occur fairly often, however, then when a major earthquake does occur it will be relatively strong because it has to relieve all the accumulated stresses. This may be very disruptive indeed. In the same way, any attempt to operate a growing and dynamic capitalist economy without even occasional moderate downswings (or at least growth recessions) is likely to face similar problems. Real economies and societies simply do not progress smoothly and without interruption, even during a *Belle Epoque.*

Probably the most important issue to consider in relation to this subject is the degree to which Say's law works, or can be made to work. Jean Baptiste Say was a nineteenth century French economist who formulated the theory that supply creates its own demand, and that unless the market is blocked it will always clear — that is, demand will equal supply, and there will be no surplus product or surplus labour. This seemingly too simple formulation has been out of fashion among economists for at least fifty years, having been replaced by the Keynesian and post-Keynesian notion that imperfections in the market need to be compensated for by increases or decreases in government spending to "assist" the market in its effort to make total demand equal total supply.

In actuality, it has proved much easier to increase government spending through deficit financing than to cut existing government services when, in theory, inflationary conditions call for decreased spending. The result is "built-in" inflation. For this reason, we believe policies would be much improved if Say's law were assumed to be basically correct, with the caveat that there are of course blocks in the system, though not in the way these blocks have traditionally been perceived. Nowadays, what was once considered a block is often considered an important and essential part of the social system. In particular, there is a down-side rigidity of price and wages due to many causes, among them:

1. trade unions, welfare payments, unemployment insurance, multiple workers per family, and a general level of affluence that makes workers normally unwilling to lower their standard of living;
2. administered prices, protected industries, and cartels that make prices especially sticky on the down-side;
3. governmentally mandated rigidities and floors, such as:
   a. price floors and price supports, for example in agriculture
   b. regulated monopolies
   c. pro-union and "closed shop" regulations

   d. import restrictions, for example, quotas, tariffs

   e. minimum wage and mandated fringe benefits;

4. various built-in escalators in wage contracts (that is, built in allowances for inflation whether it occurs or not);

5. a fear of impending price controls that sometimes contributes to an unwillingness to cut list prices;

6. an increasing share of national income accounted for by government, and thus less responsive to market pressures;

7. perhaps most important, at least in Australia, a system of setting wages through the Arbitration Commission, which, whatever its merits in times past or in terms of its utility to wage earners in the short-run, has demonstrated a tendency to pass inflationary trends through the system at a time when the economy is already severely inflation-prone.

The point here is simply to recognize that while advanced capitalist economies can provide their citizens with unparalleled affluence, as well as prospects for continued growth, such achievements cannot be without cost. In particular, groups in society cannot act as if they are entitled to support as a matter of right; society may agree to provide some floor on wages or some degree of welfare payments and unemployment insurance, but the amount of such benefits should, like other public policies, be the result of a political consensus throughout the society, and not simply among those seeking the benefits. Just as unemployment benefits arose in the first place as a result of adjustments decided upon in the wake of the travail of the Great Depression, a limitation on contemporary unemployment benefits and welfare systems is needed as an adjustment to the difficulties brought about by the persistent inflation of the 1970s.

The Asia-Pacific Context

Barring unexpected changes in current trends, the Asia-Pacific region will be the most rapidly growing area of the world for at least the next decade, and probably through the end of the century. In part, the reason is simply a stronger desire for growth.

While desire alone cannot create growth, it certainly helps — and a lack of desire impedes growth.

Japan, of course, is the model that other countries in the region are following. Even today, with a post-1973 growth rate running at only half the previous level, Japan's average growth rate remains higher than that of any other OECD country. Many Japanese and many of Japan's trading partners would warmly welcome another five to ten years of differentially higher Japanese growth. Certainly Australia would welcome it. The assumption is that such further growth would be domestic-led, and would lead in turn to a considerable increase in Japanese imports from both developed and developing countries, and of manufactured and finished goods as well as raw materials. Signs of such trends are evident in the Japanese government's most recent medium-term economic plan and in recent trade patterns subsequent to increases in the value of the yen since 1977.

Other countries in the region have also done well. All except Indonesia and the war-ravaged countries of Indochina now have per capita incomes of roughly $500 or more. They are thus no longer poor, but in a category that we label "middle-income", that is, neither poor nor affluent. All except the Indochina states are also achieving average growth rates two or three times those of most developed countries. Four resource-poor but highly motivated countries — South Korea, Taiwan, Hong Kong, and Singapore — have done particularly well, growing at average annual rates of 7 to 12 per cent (in constant 1975 prices) since 1964. These countries maintained high rates of growth even during the 1974-75 recession, and while the expected 1980-81 recession will probably lead to a sharp drop in performance, this drop is almost certain to be temporary.

Four resource-rich but less well motivated countries in the region — Malaysia, Thailand, the Philippines, and Indonesia — have grown at average annual rates of 6 to 8 per cent (in constant 1975 prices) since 1964. China, too, seems increasingly on the verge of an economic take-off. The post-Mao leadership has maintained and reaffirmed its policy of emphasizing economic development as the country's highest priority; growth from 1977 to 1979 averaged 8.7 per cent. This is a dramatic increase from the 5.7 per cent annual rate achieved in the recent past (1970 to 1976) and even more impressive when compared with the long term rate of 5.0 per cent achieved from 1957 to 1970.[25]

In general, as Ross Garnaut has noted, the potential growth of Asian countries other than Japan is likely to be as important to Australia in the 1980s as was Japan's growth in the 1960s and 1970s.[26] Somewhat upsetting to this picture of a development-oriented community of nations, China and Vietnam fought a minor war with each other in 1979, and Vietnam's domination of Kampuchea and generally pro-Soviet position casts a potentially large shadow over the region's otherwise steady emphasis on growth more than on any other goal. But even taking the Soviet-Vietnamese alliance into account, growth still seems likely to remain more important than any other single policy objective for these Asia-Pacific countries, and likely to be implemented successfully enough to continue to make this region the most rapidly growing part of the world for the rest of this century.

Indeed, if current trends continue — with the United States remaining a generally open economy, and Japan becoming more open — the various countries of the Asia-Pacific region will probably act more and more as a unit. They could become, by the mid-1980s, a trading and investment area, meaning a group of nations that send and receive at least half of their foreign trade (other than oil) and half their investments to and from each other. As these trends proceed, the nations of the region will probably try to establish some kind of formal organization. Indeed, there are moves in this direction already, although any full-fledged Pacific Community institution, which can cause things to happen rather than simply react to events that are taking place anyway, is still some years away.

The high growth rates of the Asia-Pacific region — both those that have occurred already, and those that are likely to continue occurring — create obvious opportunities for Australian economic growth. Indeed, the opportunity to link its future with other Asia-Pacific countries offers Australia a chance to take advantage of the growth of the rest of the region and "ride the wave up", in effect letting these other countries provide a population base for a wider market and a less skilled labour pool, while Australia produces *both* raw materials and manufactured goods for this widening market. However, one prerequisite for such increased exports to an ever-expanding regional market is a corresponding willingness by Australia to accept increased imports from the rest of the region. In the past, Australian manufactured goods could be produced largely for the domestic market because that market was growing and also because there were no nearby competitors. Now, as other countries in the Asia-Pacific region are producing manufactured goods of comparable or better quality and at comparable or cheaper prices, the "natural" distinctiveness of Australia as a separate market is much diminished. This climb up the value-added ladder, beginning with Japan and spreading now to every other country in the region, means that developed countries like Australia, Canada, the U.S., and Japan will have to make corresponding adjustments in their manufacturing sectors — or seek to oppose such adjustments through protectionism.

Clearly, such shifts require a considerable change in employment patterns in the developed countries, and more fundamentally, a considerable change in attitudes. In Australia's case, the kind of broad-based manufacturing sector the country has traditionally maintained, relying mainly on a small domestic market propped up by tariffs and other protectionist measures, is unlikely to be sustainable over even the medium term, since it would very likely lead other countries to take retaliatory measures. Such a manufacturing sector would almost certainly prove self-defeating in the long term, since the high internal costs generated by such a policy would eventually undermine domestic productivity even in some raw material sectors in which Australia would otherwise possess a comparative advantage.

If the Asia-Pacific region continues to be an area of more or less continuing peace and increasing prosperity, then an actively outward-looking Australian economic policy, with respect to both natural resources and manufactured goods, would have a favourable impact not only on Australia itself but also on the evolving economic and political structure of the entire region. On the other hand, if Australia were to take the view that it need not have much contact with the rest of this fast-growing region — or that it could somehow limit its contact to certain economic relationships that need not spill over into political or cultural relationships — it would risk becoming increasingly isolated and possibly even scorned. The other countries of the Asia-Pacific region will almost certainly try to maintain high growth rates to the end of the century and beyond — indeed, at least up to a point where they have achieved per capita incomes either equivalent to or higher than those prevailing in previously more developed countries. For Australia to assume that the developing countries of the region might be content with a per capita income that is distinctly (or increasingly) lower than the pace-setting level of the most advanced countries seems to us unwarranted and risky. To seek, by contrast, to participate actively in the high growth of the region as a whole is a safer, and a more admirable goal.

Notes

1. For a detailed discussion of the view that the adjustment process itself will be the dominant influence on the world economy in the 1980s, see Irving Leveson and Jimmy W. Wheeler, eds., *Western Economies in Transition: Structural Change and Adjustment Policies in Industrial Countries* (Boulder, Colo.: Westview Press, 1980).

2. Herman Kahn, William Brown and Leon Martel, *The Next 200 Years* (New York: William Morrow and Company, 1976), and Herman Kahn, *World Economic Development,* Boulder, Colo.: Westview Press, 1979).

3. See, for example, Leveson and Wheeler, *Western Economics in Transition;* Marylin Chou and David P. Harmon, Jr., eds., *Critical Food Issues Facing the 1980s* (New York: Pergamon Press, 1979); Herman Kahn and Thomas Pepper, *The Japanese Challenge: The Success and Failure of Economic Success* (Sydney: Harper & Row, 1979); William H. Overbolt, ed., *The Future of Brazil,* (Boulder, Colo.: Westview Press, 1978); Marie-Josee Drouin and B. Bruce-Briggs, eds., *Canada Has a Future* (Toronto: McClellan and Stewart Ltd., 1978); Lewis A. Dunn, *Beyond Non-Proliferation: U.S. Policy in a Proliferating World* (forthcoming, The Twentieth Century Fund); and Paul Bracken, *Arizona Tomorrow: A Precursor of Post-industrial America* (forthcoming).

4. Kahn et al, *The Next 200 Years.*

5. There was an earlier take-off period that is not discussed here.

6. Angus Maddison, "Phases of Capitalist Development", *Banca Nazionale del Lavoro Quarterly Review,* No. 121 (June 1977). The terminology Advanced Capitalist Nations is also drawn from Maddison's work.

7. A structural problem is defined as any economic problem that cannot be fixed primarily by fiscal or monetary policies (thought it is often strongly affected by these). Structural problems can involve institutional and value issues as well as structural imbalances in industries or the labour force. See

Edward M. Bernstein, "Structural Problems and Economic Policy: The U.S. Experience", in *Western Economies in Transition*, pp. 163-82.

8. This idea is drawn from Joseph Schumpeter's interpretation of long-cycles, based on a clustering of innovations. The coincidence of several major innovations triggers the use and adoption of new production systems; linkages throughout the economy then stimulate the long upswing. The microprocessor is perhaps the most impressive current innovation with the potential to stimulate pervasive growth and change. Dramatic shifts in the demographic profile of a country, caused by large changes in fertility, mortality, or migration that occur over a relatively short period of time, could also initiate investment and capital growth. Analyses of demographic forces and their impact on economic activity are associated with Simon Kuznets (particularly for pre-war periods) and Richard Easterlin (particularly for the United States since the turn of the century). See Joseph A. Schumpeter, *Business Cycles: A Theoretical, Historical, and Statistical Analysis of the Capitalist Process* (New York: McGraw-Hill, 1964); Simon Kuznets, *Secular Movements in Production and Prices* (Boston: Houghton Mifflin Co., 1930); and Richard A. Easterlin, *Population, Labor Force and Long Swings in Economic Growth* (New York: Columbia University Press, 1968).

9. This concept is also drawn from Schumpeter. In his analysis of the growth process, the creation of new, more productive processes entails some destruction of older processes.

10. In Walt W. Rostow's interpretation of long cycles in economic activity, movements of relative prices between manufactured goods and commodities are one of the most important forces leading to a topping out of growth in industrial sectors at the peak of a long cycle. See Walt W. Rostow, *The World Economy: History and Prospect* (London: The Macmillan Press Ltd., 1978).

11. The peak war concept is part of the original Kondratieff literature; it is used here primarily to characterize the occurrence of some event that crystallizes the polarization emerging in society, perhaps as a result of many forces. By itself, in other words, the peak war is more a symptom of trouble than a cause, though it does intensify the symptoms greatly. See Nikolai D. Kondratieff, "The Long Waves in Economic Life", *The Review of Economic Statistics* XVII (November 1935).

12. In the U.S. today, business has typically shortened its investment horizon from a more-or-less traditional twenty-year framework to something like five years, except in instances of obviously defensive investment. This lack of a long-term perspective is both an effect and a cause of current economic problems.

13. Chapter 4 discusses how Australia might also become an arrested industrial society.

14. Donnella H. and Dennis L. Meadows, Jorgen Randers, and William W. Behrens III, *The Limits to Growth* (New York: Universe Books, 1972).

15. Roberto Vacca, *The Coming Dark Age*, translated from the Italian by J.S. Whale (Garden City, N.Y.: Doubleday & Company, Inc., 1973).

16. Peter Schrag, *The End of the American Future* (New York: Simon and Schuster, 1973).

17. Theodore Roszak, *Where the Wasteland Ends* (Garden City, N.Y.: Doubleday & Company, Inc., 1972).

18. Charles Birch, *Confronting the Future* (Ringwood, Vic.: Penguin Books, 1976). "A way of life which has brought affluence to a third of mankind in this century," he writes in the concluding chapter, "now threatens the demise of all mankind."

19. Thorstein Veblen, *Instinct of Workmanship* (New York: Kelly, 1922), p. 347.

20. See, for example, Irving Kristol, *Two Cheers for Capitalism* (New York: Basic Books, Inc,, 1978); B. Bruce-Briggs, ed., *The New Class?* (New Brunswick, N.J.: Transaction Books 1979); Daniel Bell, *The Cultural Contradictions of Capitalism* (New York: Basic Books, Inc,, 1976); *Society*, A Symposium, "Is There a New Class?" Vol. 16, No. 2 (January/February 1979), pp. 14-62; and James T. Barry, "Welcome to the New Class", *Commonweal*, Vol. 106 (16 February 1979), pp. 73-77.

21. In principle the upper class is also affected by this shift, but because it is rich in more of an absoute sense, it is insulated from the worst effects of the change. The upper middle class is by definition not as insulated, since it competes head to head with the rising middle class.

22. The U.S hardly suffered from this, but Western Europe and Japan did. These problems affected the U.S. less severely because American investment rates had dropped sharply in the previous decade compared with Europe and Japan. This cost the U.S. a great deal in terms of lost production and lost innovation, but it did mean that when the 1974-75 recession hit, excess capacity was not as serious a problem there as it was in Europe and Japan.

23. R.G. Gregory, "Some Implications of the Growth of the Mineral Sector", *Australian Journal of Agricultural Economics* 20, no. 2 (August 1976); and "The Balance of Payments and Some Resource Allocation Issues", *Conference in Applied Economic Research* (Sydney: Reserve Bank of Australia, 1976).

24. In *The Year 2000*, a book written in the mid-1960s, one of the authors suggested that unemployment rates in the U.S. might approach 10-15 per cent by the end of the century, not because of a failure of the system, but because the success of the system would lead to considerably relaxed pressures to find and hold jobs. See Herman Kahn and Anthony J. Wiener, *The Year 2000* (New York: The Macmillan Company, 1967), especially Chapter IV.

25. Estimates of Chinese growth figures by U.S. Central Intelligence Agency, from data in various unclassified publications, and made available by personal communication.

26. Ross Garnaut, "Industrialization in Southeast and East Asia and Some Implications", in Kasper and Parry, eds., *Growth, Trade and Structural Change*, pp. 26-40, and Garnaut, ed., *ASEAN in a Changing Pacific and World Economy* (Canberra: Australian National University Press, forthcoming).

THREE

A Business-as-Usual Australia

A business-as-usual society is one that continues more or less along current lines, a society in which neither the government nor the general public makes much effort to redirect policies other than in a short-term, *ad hoc* manner. No business-as-usual future lasts indefinitely. If society does not suffer greatly from having followed policies based on short-term, *ad hoc* decisions, such a policy may be said to have succeeded. Alternatively, a business-as-usual future may last "too long", to a point where some reasonably predictable disaster or external shock occurs — and the society is suddenly forced, or willing, to make changes that it had been unable or unwilling to make before. If, despite these changes, great suffering, social unrest, or some further disaster occurs, then a business-as-usual approach may be said to have failed, in the sense of having failed to protect society from more or less predictable problems.

This chapter discusses why, in the context described in the previous chapter, and on the basis of social, economic, and political trends within Australia, a business-as-usual future seems the most likely alternative for Australia, at least to the end of this century.

Social Attitudes

As discussed in Chapter 1, the social and psychological attitudes labelled no worries, mateship and egalitarianism, and protect-my-

corner seem strong enough, relative to the countervailing influence of a striving attitude, to help make a business-as-usual
future more likely than the other alternatives. In terms of
attitudes, Australia seems likely to continue trying to pursue an
apparently safe, middle path — taking advantage of its natural
resource endowments to prop up a certain degree of self-avowed
inefficiency, and failing not only to attempt to set any records in
terms of economic growth or dynamism, but also to make even
those reforms on which there is a rough consensus.

A feeling of economic and psychological sufficiency has
become an Australian hallmark. This comfortable mood has a
basis in Australia's past performance: in the country's ever-
increasing affluence, which rose precipitously in the postwar
years even though its relative standing was falling (see Figure
3.1), and in its egalitarian distribution of income.[1] Traditionally,
Australians have felt they had a reasonable level of material
wealth and the security of an isolated continent in which to enjoy
that wealth. Relative to Western Europe, Australia has always
had a more-than-sufficient ratio of land to population. Geography
has permitted Australia to feel secure with relatively small, nonnuclear defence forces. Unlike New Zealand, with which it shares
many historical experiences, Australia has traditionally achieved
enough industrialization and enough association with the affluent
nations of the northern hemisphere to feel more or less in tune
with the rest of the world; this has produced a certain sense of
self-satisfaction with what is often described as "the basic Australian way of life". Moreover, as a predominantly Western society
located in a largely non-Western part of the world, Australia has
felt ample reason, on the basis of the usual patterns of human
history, to insulate itself from "excessive" contact with countries
of a different racial and cultural background. This is not to
endorse such isolation on either practical or moral grounds, but
simply to acknowledge that Australians, following the example of
other like-minded groups, have tended to stick together, and to
separate themselves from distinctly different groups.

Current social attitudes are promoting consolidation and
stability rather than growth and change. As David Kemp has
noted in his study of the social background to recent changes in

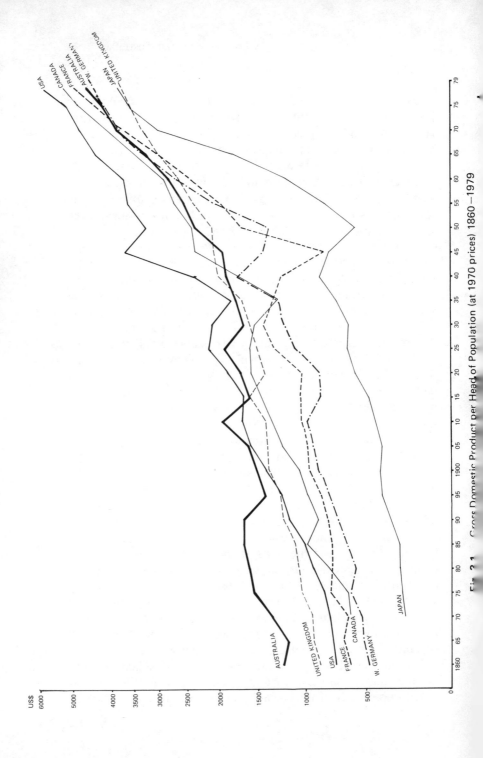

Fig. 2.1 Gross Domestic Product per Head of Population (at 1970 prices) 1860—1979

voting patterns, ... basic shifts [are] underway in the old
cleavages of class, religion, and region, and new sources of divi-
sion [are] arising".[2] Much of the working class has become middle class, meaning that its attitudes have undergone what Kemp
calls an "embourgeoisement". The absolute income of some
blue collar workers is now so high that, as a group, they have
come to adopt attitudes previously associated with white collar
workers. This middle-classing phenomenon stems mostly from
the affluence of the working class, which is caused partly by some
overlap in incomes, whereby higher paying blue collar jobs earn
substantially more than lower level white collar jobs, partly by
increased levels of education throughout the population, and
partly by the continued urbanization and/or suburbanization of
Australian living patterns.

Australia has always been more urbanized than other comparably developed countries. Nowadays, the links between major
cities are enormously reinforced by the national television net-
works, the nationally circulated newspapers, and the country's
effective, if expensive, airline routes, all of which lead to more
homogeneous tastes and fashions. Hence, old distinctions are dis-
integrating and regrouping into new ones, based largely on educational and income differences. An accountant in Adelaide has
more in common with an accountant in Brisbane than with his
neighbourhood service station mechanic, and certainly more than
with a service station mechanic in Whyalla. But all four now have
far more in common with each other than they might ever have
had before. They are all likely to own their own homes, drive
their own cars, shop at similar shopping centres, and take similar
holidays. This shift has helped tilt Australian society in general in
the direction of consolidation and stability, and away from growth
and change.

Concurrently with this middle-classing of Australian society
has come a broadened, less close-knit concept of mateship — a
change from the solidarity felt by two or three men who face
common dangers, to the alleged mateship among much larger
groups, extending beyond one region or state to the whole country. As analyzed by H.G. Oxley in his study of two rural factory
towns in New South Wales, this second concept of mateship
weakens the degree of egalitarianism felt by the larger group and

promotes stratification. In a conflict between stratification and egalitarianism, stratification is generally the stronger of the two forces, even in a mateship-conscious group.[3]

In saying that workers are becoming middle class, we are referring to a combination of many values, but not necessarily to entrepreneurial ones. For example, middle class children tend to keep their hands clean, or to be made to keep them clean, and to be oriented somewhat toward education. But this is quite different from a country's attitude towards getting ahead in the world vis-à-vis other countries. As Australians have become more affluent, they have retained their desire for high levels of protection for manufacturing, and have added new demands for welfare as a matter of right and for low levels of immigration. These demands stem from a desire to preserve the status quo. The only counter-balance comes from specific pressure groups that favour greater dynamism because they understand that economic growth is always accompanied by creative destruction.

The affluence of the postwar era has led to a change in the status of women, although how much of a change is still an open question. The "traditional" Australian family was characterized by a passive acceptance of sex roles, approval of large families, and a rejection of abortion and other kinds of family planning. A neo-progressive double standard, in which some consideration is given to the importance of changing sex roles, has gained wide currency, though traditional values remain strong. Contemporary families do tend to be smaller, but this applies to all developed countries, regardless of the status of women in their social structure. "New Class" Australians show distinctive patterns of family life, including *de facto* marriages; couples do not necessarily accept the traditional definitions of sex roles, but experiment with various patterns in search of substitutes for traditional norms. Children are a matter of choice, rather than an inevitable consequence of marriage; childbearing may come late in life in deference to other interests of either partner.

Education is a leading reason for questioning traditional norms. While such questioning is concentrated in highly educated groups, experience with conflicting norms is gradually spreading across a wide range of incomes and lifestyles. As these examples have increased and socialization patterns have changed, more women have entered the work force, and thereby become less constrained by traditional family patterns. As the number of working women grows, and the size of the family shrinks, the family as a unit is becoming more affluent. This affects job expectations, spending patterns, and discretionary choices in both work and play. For example, the desire for more leisure increases as affluence increases and working hours decrease. Strong Irish influences are evident in the most popular leisure activities in Australia — gambling, drinking and sport. Meanwhile, the boom in individuality and leisure time has expanded the whole concept of "sport" into a myriad of new pursuits.

In general, high economic growth and feelings of prosperity have fostered a widespread attitude that the era of hard work is over for Australia, and that the time for play is both plentiful and permanent — as the bumper sticker says, "I'd rather be sailing".

Demographic Issues

Australia has had two periods of particularly high population growth, 1861-1890 and 1947-1971. (See Figure 3.2.) Both periods coincided with rapid economic growth and increased immigration. Indeed, Australia could never have achieved the growth rates it did in these boom periods without increased immigration. When these booms began, the population was simply too small to provide sufficient labour to exploit the opportunities that were to appear. Moreover, Australia has been able to attract high quality immigrants whenever it needed them.

Like other developed countries, Australia experienced declines in rates of natural increase in the late nineteenth century. After fluctuations caused by two world wars and the Great Depression, rates of natural increase have again followed a generally declining trend since the late 1950s. Between 1947 and 1971, the average rate of population increase was around 2 per cent a year, which was high enough to contribute to a steadily expanding domestic market and labour supply. Nearly half of this increase came from immigration. With the onset of the worldwide recession of 1974-

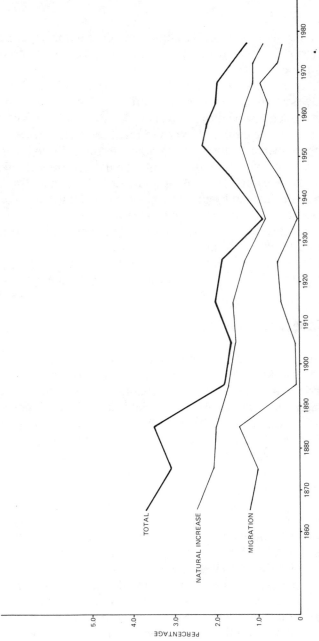

Fig. 3.2 Average Annual Rate of Population Growth (per cent), Natural Increase and Migration (Australia)
Source: *Australian Year Book*, 1979, p. 77

75, and the corresponding increase in unemployment, a consensus arose in favour of a more restrictive attitude toward immigration than had prevailed during the previous twenty-five to thirty years. Conventional expectations until the mid-1970s were that the total Australian population would be as high as twenty-five million in the year 2000, based on an average rate of population increase of 2½ per cent a year; estimates have since been scaled down to between sixteen and eighteen million, depending on the rate of immigration, but generally based on an average population growth rate of just under 1 per cent a year. The higher of these two figures assumes net immigration levels of roughly fifty thousand a year, which would represent a continuation of the average level of unassisted immigrant arrivals going back at least to 1965.[4]

The decline in rates of natural increase has created an age profile characterized by a bulge popularly known as the "baby boom". (See Figure 3.3.) Actually, Australia has two mini-bulges, which greatly complicate social planning. For example, the number of children reaching the end of compulsory schooling (age fifteen) has been declining since 1964, but this number will increase from 1981 to 1986. After 1986, it will once again decline. Thus, educational facilities have to be adjusted first to take account of a decline, then an increase, and then another decline. As such population bulges move through a life-cycle, they evolve from a "baby boom" into a "youth-and-mortgage boom", or what is sometimes separated into a youth culture era and then a nesting age era. Eventually, the bulge becomes a "pension-and-welfare boom".

Internal migration has followed a fairly clear pattern throughout the postwar period. Intrastate movements have consistently been from rural areas to the capital cities, and within that trend, from the inner cities to the surrounding suburbs. Interstate movements show a slight but steady drift in favour of Queensland and Western Australia, but it is not large enough to affect the position of either state relative to the others. Though the mining boom opened up areas in both states that had previously been virtually empty, the overall population gains occasioned by new mining activity were generally small.

Historically, Australia has had to strain — to the point of pro-

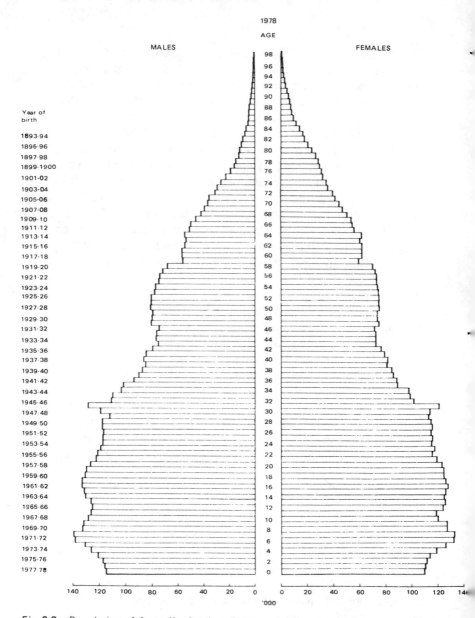

Fig. 3.3   Population of Australia, Age Last Birthday, 30 June 1978

Source: Australian Bureau of Statistics, *Estimated Age Distribution of the Population: State and Territories of Australia, 30 June 1978*, Australian Bureau of Statistics, October 1979.

viding assisted passage to migrants — to achieve a rate of population increase high enough to support a growing economy. Figure
3.4 represents a typical forecast that by the year 2000 the growth
of the labour force from domestic sources will taper off, taking
account of both low fertility rates and increased rates of female
participation in the labour force. Clearly, if such forecasts are
borne out, today's relatively high unemployment rates could
become tomorrow's labour shortage. Indeed, without increased
immigration, and taking into account a time when the second
mini-bulge enters the labour force, the total labour force might
well grow too slowly even if stagflation continues.

The immigration rate is thus the key variable in any projections

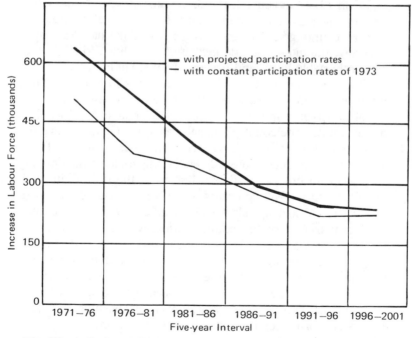

Fig. 3.4   Projected Growth of the Australian Labour Force from Domestic
Sources (Five-Year Increases)
Source: Geoff Dixon, "Resources and the National Economy in the 1980s",
in Peter Hastings and Andrew Farran (Eds.), *Australia's Resources Future* (Melbourne: Thomas Nelson Australia Pty Ltd, 1978), p. 187.

of the future Australian population, and a subject of constant
debate, much of it emotional. Australia has always had some net
immigration, although only after World War II did the ethnic
backgrounds of new immigrants begin to depart from the overwhelmingly Anglo-Celtic stock that had been dominant since the
first permanent European settlement in 1788. Beginning in 1947,
a mixture of continental Europeans dominated the new arrivals.
This changed in the 1970s; the percentage of Asians, defined to
range from Lebanese to Japanese, increased from 9.7 per cent in
1970 (18,007 out of a postwar peak total of 185,325 arriving settlers) to 32.3 per cent in 1977 (24,405 out of a total of 75,640).[5]
As well, 5,348 Indochinese refugees were admitted between 1975
and 1977. An additional 10,618 were admitted in 1978 and
14,347 in 1979.[6] In general, the percentage of new arrivals from
Asia has increased in recent years, but the total number of
arrivals (counting settlers and refugees together) has decreased.

Because the rate of natural increase has declined to a low and
apparently stable level, and because even small increases in the
absolute number of non-Caucasian immigrants show up as a pro-
portionately high increase from an extremely low base, the recent
arrival of larger numbers of Asians has created a misleading
impression that the country's racial makeup is rapidly changing.
Census data that convert these recent increases in arrivals from
Asia into a percentage breakdown of the total population by
nationality are not yet available. But given the decline in total
arrivals, compared with ten years ago, it is clear that the increased
percentage of Asian arrivals has not significantly altered the total
racial composition of the country. Moreover, it is difficult to
imagine any rate of immigration that would have more than a
marginal effect through the year 2000. A point system for judging
applications, introduced by the federal government in 1979,
together with a three-year program designed to bring in seventy
thousand immigrants net per year, aims at establishing an objective system for processing a steady flow of migrants.

The arrival of immigrants of different races or ethnic groups
has obviously required greater-than-average efforts to minimize
social tensions caused by multi-racial encounters. At the same
time, the continuation of higher-than-average unemployment

rates has strengthened opposition to immigration, regardless of race or national origin. The federal government, having begun to liberalize the White Australia policy under Prime Minister Holt in 1966 and abandoned it altogether under Whitlam in 1973, has sought under Fraser to keep Australia's doors open in spite of sluggish economic conditions — and to keep these doors open without regard to race or nationality. For example, Australia admitted a larger number of Indochinese refugees per capita than any other country in 1978 and 1979, and is fourth in the world in absolute numbers admitted since 1975. All the while, the government has sought to play down this generosity lest it trigger an even stronger public backlash than has been evident during the implementation of the policy.

As previously noted, prospective additions to the labour force from domestic sources may be insufficient to avoid a labour shortage, particularly of semi-skilled and unskilled labour, which is needed if skilled labour is to operate efficiently. In the context of Australian history, it would be perfectly normal for both government policy and public opinion to favour increased immigration if and when business conditions improve and/or a mini-resources boom creates a renewed demand for labour. The problem would arise in deciding which immigrants to pick, particularly if those seeking to immigrate turned out to be predominantly non-white.

Previous postwar increases in immigration have typically been accompanied by pleas that the pending increase be restricted to certain "desirable" groups. Almost invariably, such restrictions have proved ineffective, and new groups, initially considered "undesirable", have come in and begun making their way up the ladder to social respectability. Continental Europeans were given this back-of-the-hand treatment when they first began to arrive, and were admitted only because allegedly "exceptional" circumstances — the fears aroused by Japan's southward expansion — proved stronger than the then-prevailing prejudices of the predominantly Anglo-Celtic community. Similar criticism greeted the influx of Turks and Lebanese in the late 1960s. Looking back at this pattern, some Australians go so far as to argue that the country can never reach its full potential without an influx of immigrants as great and varied as that experienced by the United

States in the second half of the nineteenth century, leading ultimately to an Australian population as large as fifty million. Only then, the argument runs, would the social structure be sufficiently shaken up to enable the country to achieve much more than it has so far.

Clearly, a change of this magnitude would no longer constitute a business-as-usual future. Australia may well decide to limit its growth in part by limiting the degree of immigration. The choice is between lower growth and lower immigration or higher growth and higher immigration, with the distinct possibility that future immigrants would include a larger proportion of non-whites than in the past.

A second problem raised by a business-as-usual projection of immigration trends stems from the strains associated with the movement of population bulges over time. Like a possum swallowed by a carpet snake, these bulges will eventually pass through the system and disappear. But the adjustments needed to deal with them as they move along are only now beginning to be recognized, and more importantly, to be planned for in a systematic way.

For example, in the 1970s Australia's universities and colleges of advanced education enrolled about one in every six persons aged twenty, or triple the proportion enrolled during the 1950s. In 1955, Australia's universities conferred only 3,432 degrees. In 1975, the universities conferred 28,300 degrees and post-graduate diplomas; colleges of advanced education conferred an additional 24,700 degrees and diplomas.[7] In other words, during a period when the population doubled, the number of degrees and diplomas increased by 1,400 per cent. The additional educational capacity built into the system to accommodate these increases must somehow be retired or converted to more productive uses, and then brought back into operation when the second mini-bulge reaches university age.

A similar adjustment is needed in housing. By 1990, after both mini-bulges in population pass through their periods of childhood and adolescence, separate groups of the mini-bulge generation will have begun to leave their parents' homes and their parents, too, may feel the need for a different kind of housing for the last third of their lives; the market will somehow have to respond to these changes, perhaps by developing new types of structures.

If these adjustments are not made, or are made in too marginal a manner, social tensions may increase considerably. Alternatively, in a premature post-industrial or a "reformed" protectionist future, excess educational capacity might be converted from the present formal school structure into a more task-oriented educational system, incorporating more vocational training, retraining, or leisure-oriented educational opportunities. Speaking partly metaphorically and partly literally, instead of subsidizing a dying, obsolete shoe industry and many unneeded high schools, while at the same time trying to fend off a microprocessing revolution that is transforming industry in other developed and developing countries, Australia could subsidize adult education computer classes in otherwise under-utilized school buildings, which would in turn permit the shoe industry to be replaced by a microprocessing industry.

Economic Prospects

The previous chapter suggested that an *Epoque de Malaise* would afflict most wealthy countries well into the 1980s, and perhaps longer, with a normal business cycle imposed on this long cycle. In such an atmosphere, chronic stagflation would be widespread. By implication, a business-as-usual Australia would be unlikely to perform better than most other developed countries, partly because its main export products are relatively undifferentiated agricultural and industrial raw materials, whose prices are strongly affected by world demand. As economic development proceeds, consumption of such raw materials normally grows at a slower rate than the overall rate of growth. To the extent that the developed countries continued to constitute the bulk of world trade in terms of volume, Australia's exports of raw materials would tend to grow more slowly in a period of malaise than during the previous twenty-six prosperous years. If the Asia-Pacific region were to grow at a measurably higher rate than the world average, and to the extent that Australia can associate itself with this higher-than-average growth, the worldwide stagflation might affect Australia less than other countries. A mini-resource boom is a possibility, particularly if Australia's non-oil energy resources were to acquire the kind of scarcity value now associated with oil. However, in conditions of continued worldwide stagflation, a sustained boom is unlikely; even if one did occur and last a few years, it would probably not be strong enough to pull the whole Australian economy very far from a stagflation-based trend line.

Australia's record at making use of previous resource booms is mixed at best. For the last 120 years, Australia has achieved lower growth rates than an average of other comparably developed countries. Its per capita income, once the highest in the world, has slowly fallen, relative to other developed countries, since the 1890s, but particularly so in the last ten years. (See Figure 3.1.) By one landmark estimate, covering roughly a hundred-year period beginning in the 1860s, Australia's gross product per capita grew by a factor of ten, as against a factor of eighteen for the U.S., nineteen for Canada, and thirty-two for Japan.[8] Another estimate gives Australia the lowest average growth rate of developed countries subsequent to their so-called "take-off".[9] A still more recent estimate of long-term growth trends ranks Australia first among sixteen advanced capitalist countries in terms of product per capita in 1870, fourth as late as 1969, but eighth in 1974-78.[10] Figure 3.5 shows that Australia's total output grew at relatively high rates between 1860 and 1890, but at low rates, compared with other developed countries, from 1890 all the way through to 1947, when output once again grew rapidly, though not quite to the level attained in the nineteenth century. The high growth rates of total output in the postwar period, which are due at least in part to a much increased rate of immigration as well as to the resources boom of the late 1950s and 1960s varied from an average growth rate of 3 per cent from 1947 to 1960 to an average of 4 per cent from 1960 to 1974, followed by a drop to an average of 2.7 per cent from 1973 to 1979.

The highest rates of growth in Australian history have come when a rapidly expanding population was developing new land or newly discovered resources, and doing so at a time when the economy of the rest of the world was expanding at a similarly fast

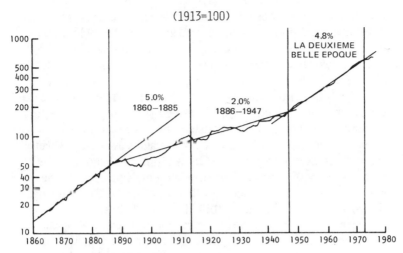

Fig. 3.5   An Index of Australian Output, with Estimated Annual Percentage Growth Rates
Source: A. Maddison, "Phases of Capitalist Development", *Banca Nazionale Del Lavoro Quarterly Review*, (June 1977), and Organization for Economic Co-operation and Development.

pace. But in the context of Australia's average long-term growth pattern, the relatively high growth rates achieved between 1960 and 1974 seem likely to be no more than a brief interlude in an otherwise slow decline — at least in the absence of a decided improvement in current trends.

During the 1950s and 1960s, the growth in Australia's total product was slightly above the OECD average, but growth in product per capita was lower than the OECD average.[11] In other words, Australia's postwar growth relied much more on increases in factor inputs — population, land in use, and employed capital — than on increases in productivity. The work force, for example, expanded almost twice as fast as in other OECD countries, while the average increase in product per worker was only half the OECD average.[12] In fact, the increases in factor inputs were considerably higher than comparable increases in other developed countries, while the reallocation of resources and increased use of technology that normally accompanies economic growth were considerably below those in other developed countries. This lack of reallocation during a period of high growth not only limited the rate of growth, but also represented an extraordinary lost opportunity to restructure the economy relatively painlessly. Indeed, this is exactly the point. When things are going well, Australia's liking for the status quo means there is no great pressure to restructure the economy; when the recession finally occurs, the pressures that then arise are considerably more painful.

As in other developed countries, Australia's agricultural sector has declined as a percentage of Gross Domestic Product (GDP) in terms of both output and employment, but the decline in employment has been much less than in other OECD countries. The reallocation of labour within the manufacturing sector has also been less, with newly arriving immigrants distributing themselves pretty much along existing industrial lines, at the lower end of the scale.[13] Australia's traditional protectionism, however beneficial in helping "infant industries" get established, has continued to the point of actively discouraging innovation and preventing the sort of structural change under way in other less protectionist environments. Thus, even during the most dynamic period of Australia's postwar growth, when labour, land, and capital were all expanding rapidly, the inter-sectoral structure of the economy did not change appreciably, and, in particular, previous patterns of manufacturing did not change much at all. To be sure, a much-expanded mining industry was added to the overall Gross National Product (GNP), but mining provides only a small additional contribution to employment. Indeed, the contribution that mining has made to GNP and to total exports has helped mask the relatively static, and decreasingly competitive, nature of Australia's manufacturing sector.

Recovery since the 1974-75 recession has been gradual and uneven. As the most recent OECD survey of Australia noted in this regard, "the growth of output has stemmed at different times from different demand components, none of which have risen consistently fast".[14] Fraser's government has sought first to bring down the rate of inflation, and with it the rate of growth of real wages. During the years of Labor party government wages had risen at a much higher rate than productivity, constituting a major

cause of Australia's 15 per cent inflation rate in 1974-75. Under
Fraser's plan, market forces will react both naturally and
positively as excess inflation (including the so-called "wage over-
hang") is gradually squeezed out of the system. Investment will
pick up, and with it the competitiveness of Australian manufacturing, which would then serve as a basis for increased employment, increased exports, and high and sustainable growth over
the medium-to-long-term.

Though endorsed by such outside observers as the OECD
Review Committee and the Economist Intelligence Unit, this
approach admittedly carries with it a considerably higher rate of
unemployment than Australia has traditionally considered normal. Not surprisingly, this is precisely the point the Labor opposition has chosen to emphasize. It argues that unemployment rates
of 5 per cent or more are an intolerable price to pay, even in the
short-term, for whatever medium and long-term benefits might
be derived from a gradual decline in inflation. Hence, the opposition says that if it were elected, it would increase public spending
and attempt to increase aggregate demand even if this results in
higher inflation.

The arguments of both the government and the opposition
assume, at least implicitly, that Australia's less-than-average
growth record since the 1974-75 recession has been caused as
much by external as internal factors. Both arguments also assume
that if world demand were to return to previously customary
levels, say by the early 1980s, the performance of the Australian
economy would improve as a matter of course. Indeed, 1979 was
a good year for Australian optimists. Real GDP rose some 4 per
cent; the Sydney All Ordinary Stock Exchange, buoyed in part by
new mineral discoveries in the Kimberlies and Roxby Downs,
rose more than four hundred index points, almost a 50 per cent
increase on the year; and the Iranian Revolution made
Australia's non-oil energy resources and relative political stability
suddenly look more attractive to foreign investors. As a result, it
has become even easier to believe that fears of alleged underlying
structural deficiencies in the Australian economy are in fact less
damaging than various Cassandras have been suggesting. In this
frame of mind, Australians might easily think they are destined

for another lucky break, even though the rest of the world may be unlucky. Even if these expectations may be justified to some degree, it would still be important to exploit vigorously whatever opportunities exist.

Nonetheless, such an attitude has to place extraordinary reliance on luck. It says, in effect, that Australia can do well — or at least "well enough" — either because world demand will soon pick up, or because there will be disruptions overseas in the supply of goods in which Australia has a comparative advantage. The precedent for the first contingency is the experience of the minerals boom, when the country prospered without apparently having to make conscious changes in its social structure or its avowedly relaxed way of doing business. Australians found minerals in such vast quantities, and sold them so effortlessly, that a repetition of this course of events comes immediately to mind, in line with the "lucky country" argument. The precedent for the second contingency is the so-called "wool boom" of the Korean War when a cold weather war led to increased wool exports.

Precedent or no precedent, in looking at Australia's long-term growth trend and at the world and historical context in which Australia finds itself, such good luck hardly seems likely to recur indefinitely. To assume that increases in world demand will be large enough to pull Australia back up to its peak postwar growth rates of 4 per cent a year or higher is to assume either a return to the kinds of world growth rates characteristic of a *Belle Epoque*, or a great increase in Australia's share of world markets. While neither possibility is completely out of the question, neither seems likely. To assume that Australia can uniquely benefit from chaotic world supply conditions seems even less prudent, especially since any such supply disruptions would have to be small enough not to precipitate a world depression but still big enough (and long enough) to let Australia enjoy windfall profits.

Moreover, even assuming some pickup in world demand, various macro-economic indicators within Australia cast doubt on the likelihood that a business-as-usual approach would achieve the successful adjustments that its proponents expect. For example, though inflation fell from a one-month peak of 17 per cent in 1974 to a 9.6 per cent annual rate in 1979, it is expected to rise to 10 per cent in 1980 and in any case has not yet fallen to an absolute level low enough to insulate the economy from a renewed surge of inflationary pressures. Similarly, profits and wages as a share of GDP have moved toward a return to tra-ditional levels without, in the case of profits, having moved far enough to stimulated renewed investment, except perhaps in energy and energy-related industries. The balance of payments also improved in 1978 and 1979, having moved toward the pat-tern established during the mineral boom, when a current account deficit was covered by private capital inflows, mostly resource investments: these inflows would continue only if world demand for such resources were sustained.

Various structural, or micro-economic, factors point to an even more serious set of problems. To the extent that a full-scale recovery of the Australian economy depends upon an increased competitiveness in the manufacturing sector, the record to date either in reducing levels of protection or in seeking and obtaining new export markets for manufactured goods is questionable at best. Even so cautious a group as the OECD review committee could not avoid noting that the Australian government's policy of continuing a relatively high level of protection for manufacturing conflicts head-on with the government's theoretical policy on manufacturing outlined in the 1977 White Paper. As the latest OECD survey put it:

> While this [conflict] is recognized and the temporary increase in pro-
> tection has probably helped to slow down the fall in employment in
> the highly protected industries, there have inevitably been associated
> costs . . . The longer-run costs of protective measures are . . . con-
> siderable and it is obviously desirable that they should be replaced as
> soon as possible by measures encouraging structural adjustment and
> greater efficiency.[15]

In effect, by talking about structural adjustment without actually doing much about it, government policy has assumed implicitly that the positive effects of a pickup in world demand would not only stimulate further development of Australia's mineral resources (and with it a greater capital inflow), but also that this pickup would be so great as to allow Australia to operate a decreasingly competitive manufacturing sector virtually indefinitely.

This is a big assumption, particularly when compared to the systematic industrial development policies of most other countries in the Asia-Pacific region. Already, Australia is the least dynamic industrial economy in the world's most economically dynamic region. Japan, South Korea, Taiwan, Singapore, and even Hong Kong — a British colony that until four years ago did not generally think of itself as having much of a future — have all taken steps to acquire modern, efficient industrial plants that serve world markets. Even some of the less industrialized countries of the region, notably Malaysia, Thailand, and the Philippines, have acquired new plants and processes in some areas of their manufacturing sectors. These countries can now compete in many product lines which Australia was once able to produce without fear of regional competition. Their spectacular successes in developing increasingly efficient and sophisticated manufacturing sectors is now common knowledge in Australia, without, however, leading to much change in Australian behaviour, particularly at the level of government policy.

Alongside the inefficiencies caused by continued protection of manufacturing, the Australian economy is also hampered by having one of the most disputatious labour forces in the world. Slightly more than half the work force is unionized, as against an OECD average of 38.5 per cent, and the trade union structure consists of a large number of relatively small, and often highly factionalized, units. This makes intra-union jurisdictional disputes at least as important a part of labour-management relations as disputes between labour on one side and management on the other. Australia's unique system of compulsory arbitration has traditionally included an explicit goal of warding off disputes, even at the price of higher wage settlements. Critics therefore contend that the system has a built-in bias toward inflationary wage settlements. Indeed, even with such a system — critics would say because of this system — Australia has far and away more disputes per worker than other comparably developed countries (see Figure 3.6); in terms of working days lost, it is not

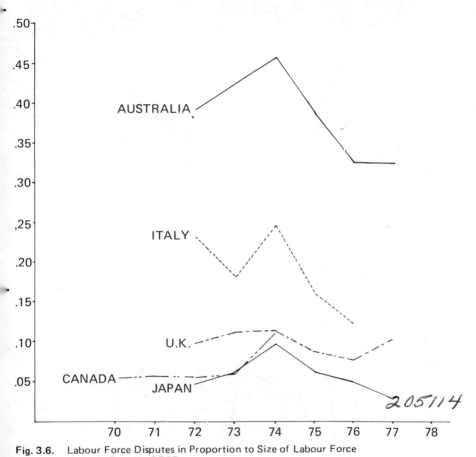

.50
.45
.40 AUSTRALIA
.35
.30
,25   ITALY
.20
.15
.10   U.K.
.05 CANADA
           JAPAN   205114

     70   71   72   73   74   75   76   77   78

Fig. 3.6. Labour Force Disputes in Proportion to Size of Labour Force
Sources: Labour Force — OECD
             Disputes in Australia — Year Book 1979, p. 156, 160.
             For Canada — Year Book 76—77.
             Disputes in U.K., Italy, Japan
             Ministry of Labour, *Labour Disputes Statistics*
             International Labour Office, *Yearbook of Labour Statistics.*
             Department of Employment, U.K., *Department of Employment Gazette.*

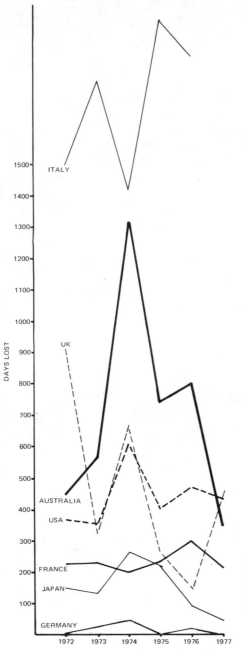

Fig. 3.7 Working days lost per 1,000 employees (all causes)

Source: United Nations World Tables 1978

as bad as Italy but worse than Britain (see Figure 3.7). Without resorting to explanations based on "national character", this poor record can certainly be attributed, in part, to the multiplicity of individual unions and their lack of coordination or cooperation.

From the point of view of a foreign enterprise that is considering whether to invest in Australian resource development or in competing countries such as Canada, Brazil, or Jamaica, the reliability of the labour force is certainly a major determining factor. In a highly capital-intensive sector such as mining, where investments are sometimes measured in units of billions of dollars, the likelihood of frequent, even if short, production shutdowns or shipping stoppages is at the very least disconcerting. Studies of industrial relations, such as Stephen Frenkel's investigation of industrial conflict in the Pilbara, suggest that part of the problem is not so much militant unions as weak unions, which lack the strength to perform the function designated for them at the workplace, and turn as a result to political action or politicized industrial relations. "The failure of management and unions to support and encourage strong workplace union organizations has led", Frenkel says, "to an organizational vacuum at site level. This has largely been filled by autonomous sectional industrial action."[16] The lack of organization — starting at the most basic level, with poorly trained shop stewards who have little sway over their more rebellious peers — leads to "an enduring stream of frequent, small-scale, short duration, grievance-intensive stoppages."[17] Frenkel also contends that rigid attitudes on the part of management, combined with an insufficient delegation of authority in labour-management negotiations, leads to a degree of dissension and divisiveness that rivals that of the unions.

This points to a dilemma. However unhappy businessmen may be with Australia's habit of frequent lightning strikes by small, fractious unions, they have traditionally been downright fearful of the potential power that might be held by a few giant unions. Larger, responsible unions, as advocated by many trade union executives, could clearly be a great improvement over the existing system, but it is at least an open question as to whether such large unions would in fact act as responsibly as their proponents claim.

As noted in Figures 3.6 and 3.7, both the number of disputes
and the number of working days lost fell back after the 1974-75
recession, which suggests that some self-correcting forces were at
work. However, the number of working days lost rose significantly in 1979, suggesting that a trend for the better has not yet
developed. Hence, it would be difficult to discount completely
previous scepticism as to whether industy-wide unions would
constitute an improvement over the current system — whether,
for example, such large organizations would have a better understanding of inflation and the effects of indexation on inflation.
Clearly, the trade union movement has felt itself under greater
pressure since the 1974-75 recession, but is just as clearly unsure
which direction to take. Moreover, continuing power struggles
between leftist and centrist factions within the union movement
and the Labor party hardly suggest that a new consensus will be
easy to formulate.

Under these circumstances, the Australian economy in a business-as-usual future could be characterized for the next decade or
two in roughly the following terms:

- From the perspective of an outside customer, it would continue to be a major supplier of raw materials — mainly iron
  ore, coal, bauxite/alumina, uranium, and natural gas. But few
  uniquely attractive manufactured goods seem likely candidates
  for export.

- From the perspective of a foreign investor, it would present
  reasonably attractive opportunities for joint venture projects,
  particularly in mineral and energy development, but truculent
  labour unions and erratically formulated government regulations would continue to act as persistent sources of risk.

- From the perspective of an outside marketer, the economy
  would remain relatively small, distant, marginal, and highly
  protectionist. Concessions to foreign exporters would be given
  mainly to those nations that purchase Australia's principal
  exports.

From the perspective of an average Australian, the economy
would continue to grow at relatively unexceptional rates, and to
operate "well enough" with a combination of protected indus-

tries, disruptive unions, modest returns on investment, and continuing government interference. And for a while longer at least, the life-style would be generally agreeable, the pace comfortable, and the cares of the world remote.

Domestic Politics

Like most other democracies today, Australia seems in the midst of a neo-conservative shift in domestic politics. The term "neo-conservative" is used to emphasize the relative nature of the shift: in Australia, as elsewhere, this trend is as much a reaction to an earlier shift — toward greater government involvement in the economy and a corresponding rise in taxes — as it is a positive assertion of a traditionally conservative political philosophy. The shift is evident first in terms of election results, which have generally favoured conservative parties in almost all democracies over the past five years. It is also evident in the rise of tax revolt and deregulation campaigns in the United States and elsewhere, and in an actual decline in the ratio of government expenditures to GDP in a number of countries (see Figure 3.8).

As previously mentioned in connection with long-cycle theories, this reappearance of traditional values seems related to a downturn in economic activity. If a long period of good times leads to a build-up of bad habits — speculative excesses, self-indulgent political movements, nihilistic art — then the arrival of bad times leads to, or coincides with, a reaffirmation of traditional values. However, long-term trends in all emerging post-industrial societies point toward an increased emphasis on welfare, leisure, and consumption, and a decreased emphasis on growth, investment, and market efficiency as the main criteria of economic decisions. By implication, no neo-conservative shift, no matter how strong, can reverse these long-term trends. Rather, the most such a shift can do is to slow down the pace at which emerging post-industrial societies take on these otherwise inevitable characteristics. How fast this pace will be in a country like Australia can be gauged only in terms that are either very general or very dependent on concrete circumstances of the moment: for example, would Bob Hawke's entry into federal politics greatly

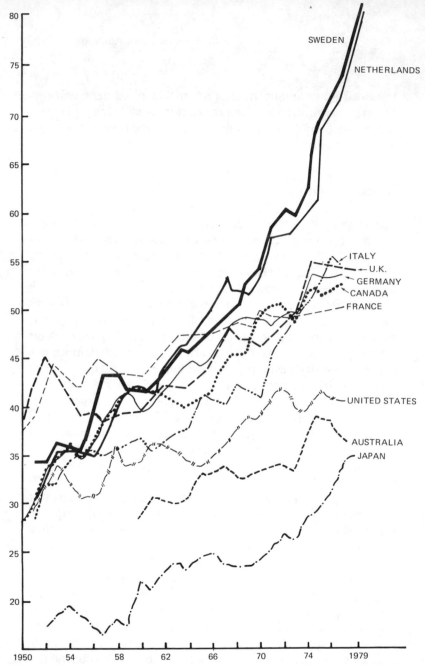

Fig. 3.8 Government Expenditures as a Percentage of National Income: Selected OECD Countries 1950–1979

Source: National Accounts of OECD Countries, Volume 11, OECD, 1979.

affect the future patterns of competition between the Australian Labor party and the Liberal/Country party coalition?

In general terms, the analysis David Kemp put forth — that Australia's traditionally egalitarian income distribution meant that a class basis for political differences was never as strong as it may have seemed to politicians — is even more relevant in recent years than, say, in the days of such dominating personalities as H.V. Evatt or Sir Robert Menzies.[18] Throughout the postwar period, with its precipitous rise in absolute levels of affluence, the earlier absence of strong income distinctions merged with an increasingly strong middle-classing effect. This led to a drift of blue-collar voters (both urban and rural) toward the more conservative parties. Simultaneously, the rise of mass media, particularly television, contributed to a decline in the influence of the traditional party organizations, and in turn to a drift of white-collar and upper middle-class professionals to the ALP and to splinter protest parties that crop up more easily as grass-roots organizations become less important.

Although Kemp's conclusions go no further than this, he stresses that both the ALP and the Liberal and Country parties are likely to run into trouble as their traditional bases of support change; this implies that even greater change is in store in the future. Lacking the reliable support base of the past, all Australian parties will now have to renew their ever more ephemeral links to voters more often, more visibly, and — because of television — more symbolically. In short, strong individual leaders will be needed, for better or worse, simply to bring a party to victory. In the longer-term, even if it maintains a parliamentary system, Australia will be adopting aspects of a strong presidential system of the sort now associated with the U.S. and France.[19] Instead of a seemingly stable contest between a "permanently" rural/business group on one side and a "permanently" labour-oriented group on the other, these trends suggest a shift toward ever-increasing competition among various centrist-inclined parties.

In this case, many new and previously unimaginable coalitions become possible, depending upon a much larger swinging vote than in the past. Indeed, swinging voters are probably more important in Australia than in other parliamentary democracies because of the requirement for compulsory voting. By way of example, two strong West German Social Democrats, Willy Brandt and Helmut Schmidt, were able to move their party to the right and thereby given it a broader appeal. The Social Democrats held onto their labour support and attracted the Free Democrats, a party supported by small business, into a new coalition, leaving the conservative Christian Democrats in a minority. In the U.K., the Labour party victory in 1974 and the Conservative party victory in 1979 can be attributed to the ability of both parties to attract sufficient numbers of swinging voters. Similarly in the U.S., both the Republican and Democratic parties suffered egregious defeats when each nominated "extremists" — Senator Barry Goldwater in 1964 and Senator George McGovern in 1972. Correspondingly, each party won in 1968 and 1976, if only barely, when their respective presidential candidates were able to convince the electorate that their version of centrism was preferable to that of the other party.

What are the implications of this centrist trend in Australia under a business-as-usual future? The first implication is already evident in the initial neo-conservative reaction to the Whitlam years — namely, a continuation of the centrist trend as long as economic conditions remain relatively depressed. If the Laor party were to move to the right, at either the federal or state level, or both, it could well capture this neo-conservative reaction in much the same way as the Social-Democratic party did in Germany. Alternatively, if the Labor party were to veer left, then the Liberal/Country party coalition could be expected to remain in power at the federal level, and at most state levels, for as long as a neo-conservative trend continued.

If world demand were to turn up, then the underlying conditions favouring a stability-oriented party would diminish. In those circumstances, the ALP might do better regardless of whether it consciously turned to the right; however, its prospects would probably still be improved if it were to move right rather than left. But at some point in a period of good times, the ALP might gain support in much the same way as it did in 1972: by appealing to the notion that it was a time for change, that the stability of a Liberal/Country government had run its course.

Indeed, to the degree that a Liberal/Country party coalition succeeds in restoring stability to the system, it sows the seeds of an eventual counter-reaction, in which voters seek to consume a greater share of the prosperity their recent investment in stability has brought them. Other things being equal, by pulling all parties toward the centre, the neo-conservative trend reinforces a business-as-usual future; in the absence of a conscious decision to seek either "reformed" protectionism or economic dynamism, the centrist trend is one of minimum risk, that is, business-as-usual. During conditions of stagflation, this neo-conservative trend can temporarily neutralize an otherwise long-term trend toward adoption of post-industrial values. Thus, as prosperous times return, pressures also mount for a shift to an early post-industrial future.

Foreign Relations

Australia has long since put an end to "Mother Country" relations with Britain. It remains allied to, and dependent upon, the United States, but much less deferentially than in times past. The idea is now generally accepted that, if Australia belongs to any grouping of countries, it belongs most of all to a diverse, vaguely defined community of nations in the Asia-Pacific region. Shifting trade patterns, as shown in Figure 3.9, are the major cause of this change in Australian perceptions of the country's place in the world. Considerable discussion of this point has of course taken place in Australia ever since the end of World War II — generally revolving around the question of whether, and how, Australia might gain by linking its economic and defence policies more closely to those of other countries in the region.

Indeed, most countries' foreign policies are now strongly linked to changes in economic policy. The tremendous expansion of world trade that occurred between 1947 and 1973 led in turn to the development of a virtually one-world market, whose impact on Australia has now become even greater than the impact of economic changes that were also taking place during this period within Australia. While the boom of the late 1960s raised the country's standard of living, it did so only by linking Australia's

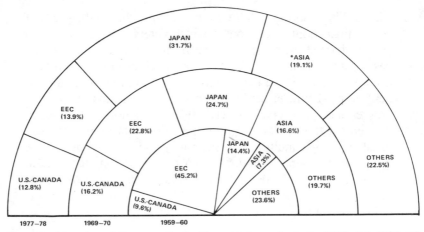

Fig. 3.9 Direction of Overseas Trade (Exports) from Australia, 1959–60, 1969–70, 1977–78

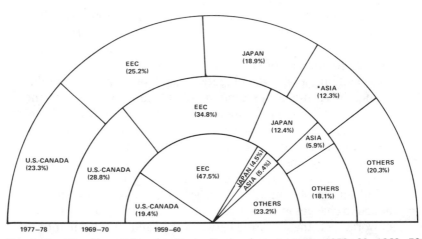

Fig. 3.10 Direction of Overseas Trade (Imports) to Australia, 1959–60, 1969–70, 1977–78

Sources: *Australian Year Book* 1971, p. 298 and *Australian Year Book* 1979, p. 591.

*Asia in this case refers to: Papua New Guinea, Indonesia, Singapore, Malaysia, Thailand, Philippines, China, Hong Kong, Taiwan, and South Korea.

prosperity to that of other countries more strongly than ever before.

Thus, Australia has come, like other countries, to the position of having little choice but to take a more-or-less outward-looking approach to foreign relations. Australia can no longer fashion its own economic policies without taking careful account of the economic policies of others. Moreover, the slowdown in overall economic growth rates since 1974 has made the high growth rates of the Asia-Pacific region increasingly important for Australia — and for the rest of the world as well. China's new economic pragmatism and the threat of protectionism in other developed countries, particularly in Western Europe, are additional reasons for Australia to pay closer attention to relations with Asian-Pacific countries.

In the past, a nation's foreign and defence policies were often based on axiomatic principles. Some legacy of this system remains even now. For example, throughout history there has never been a treasure house of resources as undefended as the Persian Gulf is today. Basically, the oil-rich nations are defended less by military hardware than by the rules of the international system itself, which of course stem from a nuclear balance between the U.S. and the Soviet Union, but which also stem from the self-restraint built up as a result of that balance. This is why the Soviet invasion of Afghanistan was such an issue for the world. It broke a tradition of respecting boundaries, which is the same tradition that has brought pressure on Israel to return to its pre-1967 boundaries and that has refused to sanction the Vietnamese invasion of Kampuchea. And, as noted in the previous chapter, it is hard to see how this tradition can continue unless the U.S. takes measures to make itself unequivocally stronger than the Soviet Union.

Australia, in this context, is slowly becoming something like the Persian Gulf — a vast storehouse of natural resources that may at some point become a target. At that point, its foreign relations, alliances, military capabilities, and efficiency and morale would become extremely important in any calculations about its future. Clearly, Australia can no longer follow its once-traditional policy of simply supporting, and relying upon, a protecting power

— first Britain, and later the U.S. Rather, it must make its own calculations of foreign policy.

Still, a country with as small a population and as large a territory as Australia would have great difficulty defending itself single-handedly. To do so would require even greater efforts in terms of budgets and people than those made by countries like Sweden and Switzerland. Typically, the safer and more feasible course for a small country is to ally with at least one major power, and to develop close relations with as many neighbouring countries as mutual interests permit. This, in fact, has been the course Australia has followed since World War II — firstly, through the ANZUS alliance and continuing support of American policies; secondly, through contributions to various British Commonwealth defence agreements with Malaysia and Singapore; and all along through a consistent policy of letting pragmatic considerations, rather than ideologies of either the right or the left, dominate relations with Indonesia.

Australia has a long-standing fear of isolation, in that it is a predominantly Caucasian parliamentary democracy, on a largely empty continent, in a non-white region of the world with predominantly authoritarian governments. This fear of isolation is probably much less justified if other countries in the region are busily pursuing policies that emphasize economic growth, and Australia is participating in this same drive for further growth at something resembling their pace — or at least not falling too far behind. That would enable both Australia and its neighbours to share the benefits of a growing pie rather than fight over slices of a static pie. Indeed, this is probably the most reassuring image of the future of the region that one could imagine.

Another, and more traditional, image would include the possibility that Indonesia or some other early industrializing Asian country might become bellicose, either as a result of excess energies or simply as a by-product of its dynamism as it industrializes. This was certainly a common pattern for early industrializing countries in the nineteenth and early twentieth centuries.

On the other hand, the past need not be a guide to future events if the Great Transition operates — as well it might — bringing all countries to a position of relatively equal wealth, with relatively fewer reasons for conflict than in the past. Australia, as an emerging post-industrial society, can leave the matter open, but precisely because it is an open question, Australia might favour higher rather than lower growth rates, greater rather than lesser technological and manufacturing capabilities, and a serious defence capability to insure itself against the worst contingencies. It is safer to prepare for the worst and not have to face it than to take the opposite course of hoping for the best but finding that it does not happen.

For the moment, however, if Australia's foreign and defence policies are determined mainly by economic issues, then the effectiveness of an outward-looking approach to the Asia Pacific region depends on how successfully the Australian economy — and specifically the manufacturing sector — is able to adjust to changes taking place abroad. As noted earlier, the record to date either in reducing levels of protection on imported manufactured goods or in obtaining new export markets for Australian manufactured goods is discouraging at best. A recent study of Australia's relations with developing countries made this same point:

> . . . the question is whether we can continue indefinitely to postpone decisions on serious action to implement the undertaking in the White Paper on the Manufacturing Industry to progress towards a lower and more stable tariff. Can we ignore the adverse effects on our economic position in the region of continuing to use our resources in ways that are inhibiting our longer term growth prospects? Can we overlook the adverse effects on our political and economic relations with our developing neighbours arising from the contradiction between our continuing rhetoric of regional friendship and cooperation and our failure to move to improve the access of these countries to our markets?[20]

The study went on to argue that, far from seeking to isolate itself from the consequences of industrialization in developing countries, Australia should "set out deliberately and energetically to facilitate the transition to a more outward-looking Australian industrial structure".[21] In other words, where earlier government-commissioned studies on the manufacturing industry had

concluded that Australia's industrial structure could not be fruit-
fully discussed without also considering various economic
changes going on in other countries, this more recent study concluded that Australia's relations with other countries could not be
discussed without also considering changes in Australia's
industrial structure. This symmetry is more than a bureaucratic
tactic. It represents a growing realization, at least at the level of
consensus-seeking government study committees, that domestic
policy and foreign policy are so closely interrelated as to be virtually inseparable, and that problems of structural change are
central to both.

Immigration policy is another issue where the connection between domestic and foreign policy is unmistakable. The federal
government abandoned the White Australia policy only when it
became indefensible on foreign policy grounds. Coincidentally, it
abandoned the old policy at roughly the point when economic
growth in other countries in the Asia-Pacific region had begun to
accelerate so much that pressures for emigration from those
countries were in fact decelerating. Hence, the traditional Australian fear that some over-populated Asian country, bursting at its
seams, would invade the continent to acquire empty land in
which to settle millions of people is no longer as plausible as it
may once have seemed. And with the prospective economic
growth of Australia's Asian neighbours greater now than at any
time in the past, such a dramatic resettlement of large numbers of
people will remain relatively unlikely. Meanwhile, the contempt
that Australians had for the poverty that once characterized Asia
will continue to diminish as these nations gradually grow richer.
Australian attitudes towards the Japanese are the best example to
date of how wealth does change otherwise "fundamental"
attitudes: Australians still fear a strong Japan, but also respect a
rich Japan.

Australia's foreign relations are not characterized by a single
cohesive policy towards other countries, but consist of various
conflicting policies competing for dominance. As the recent study
on relations with developing countries noted:

> . . . Much of our friction with the ASEAN countries resulted as much
> from unresolved and generally unrecognized conflicts among our

own interests as from a conflict between their interests and ours . . .
   What conclusions we would reach on these issues would depend
more than anything else on how we answered some long-standing
questions about Australia itself and its future as a country.[22]

A business-as-usual projection, in which society continues more
or less along current lines, might be summarized as follows: in
terms of social attitudes, Australians remain satisfied, even com-
placent; they prefer stability and less hassle to growth and
more hassle — to share what they have among a smaller population rather than increase what they might produce with a larger
population. In terms of economic performance, Australia grows
at a slower rate than other countries in the Asia-Pacific region,
but at a rate high enough to satisfy most Australians; the country
continues to slip in terms of its rank in per capita income, but not
so much that the decline leads to a concerted effort to reverse this
drift. There is, in other words, considerable resource development, and some manufacturing development, but inefficiencies
are permitted — even encouraged — to a point where they
hamper the growth potential of both the resource and the
manufacturing sector. In domestic politics, complacency in social
attitudes reinforces a middle-class conservatism, discouraging
either a sharp turn to the left or a sharp turn toward "reformed"
protectionism or economic dynamism. Foreign relations continue
to be more outward-looking than before, but not enough to
satisfy Australia's harder-working neighbours.
   Because its productivity gains have been lower than they could
or would have been if the economy had been more open,
Australia's potential for future gains is that much greater. But in a
business-as-usual future, policies and attitudes continue more or
less as before, and Australians fail to take the steps required to
produce such gains — or even to insure themselves against down-
side risks. Slowly, but only slowly, the country continues to
become less competitive, and eventually less able to control its
own destiny. Since the decline is so slow in coming, it is that
much more difficult to recognize and to deal with. Indeed,

because Australia is at the moment so much wealthier than its neighbours, and so well endowed with natural resources, it could even do well under a business-as-usual future — at least for the next five years, or at least "well enough" to satisfy most Australians. The issue, then, is how well, or how carefully, to live in the near-to-medium term as against the medium-to-long term.

Notes

1. See Malcolm Sawyer, *Income Distribution in OECD Countries* (Paris: OECD Occasional Studies, July 1976).
2. D.A. Kemp, *Society and Electoral Behaviour in Australia* (St Lucia: University of Queensland Press, 1978), p. xviii and *passim.*
3. H.G. Oxley, *Mateship in Local Organization* (St Lucia: University of Queensland Press, 1978), *passim,* esp. chapter 2.
4. See National Population Inquiry, *First Report* (1975) and *Supplementary Report* (1978), and *Australian Immigration,* Consolidated Statistics No. 10, 1978 (Canberra: AGPS) and Australian *Year Book* (Canberra: Australian Bureau of Statistics, 1979).
5. *Year Book,* 1979, p. 101. The proportion of European immigrants (excluding New Zealanders) dropped from 77.8 per cent in 1970 to 41.9 per cent in 1977; the proportion from Britain and Ireland from 41.8 per cent to 28.3 per cent.
6. Refugee figures from U.N. High Commissioner for Refugees. As of November 1979, this total of 30,313 Indochinese refugees admitted since 1975 included 2,217 "boat people" in fifty-three boats. (Australian Consulate General, New York).
7. National Population Inquiry, *Supplementary Report,* p. 97.
8. Simon Kuznets, *Economic Growth of Nations* (Cambridge, Mass.: Harvard University Press, 1971), Chapter 1, *passim.*
9. Walt W. Rostow, "Growth Rates at Different Levels of Income and Stage of Growth: Reflections on Why the Poor Get Richer and the Rich Slow Down" (University of Texas at Austin: processed, undated, received 1978), *passim.*
10. Angus Maddison, "Per Capita Output in the Long Run", *Kyklos,* Vol. 32 (1979), pp. 412-429. See also his "Phases of Capitalist Development", *Banca Nazionale del Lavoro Quarterly Review,* No. 121 (June 1977).
11. *OECD, Economic Survey of Australia,* 1972, p. 22.
12. See David H. Robertson, "Australia's Growth Performance: An Assessment", in Kasper and Parry, eds., *Growth, Trade and Structural Change, passim.*
13. Ibid., p. 80. See also Industries Assistance Commission, *Structural Change in Australia* (Canberra: AGPS, 1977).
14. *OECD, Economic Survey of Australia,* 1979, p. 7.
15. Ibid., pp. 40, 45.
16. Stephen Frenkel, *Industrial Conflict in the Pilbara Iron Ore Industry: A Preliminary Investigation,* Australia-Japan Economic Relations Research Project, Research Paper No. 54, October 1978, p. 17.
17. Ibid., p. 14.

18. See Kemp, *Society and Electoral Behaviour*, especially Chapter 10.
19. The term "strong presidential system" refers to a system in which a single chief executive, who is both head of government and head of state, is directly elected in a nation-wide poll, as against a non-monarchical parliamentary system, in which a weak president serves as head of state but not head of government, as in West Germany, Italy, Ireland and Israel. Australia might adopt aspects of a strong presidential system in a *de facto* sense, without changing its formal government structure at all.
20. Report of *The Committee on Australia's Relations with the Third World* (Canberra: AGPS, 1979), p. 131.
21. Ibid., p. 131.
22. Ibid., p. 127 and 129.

FOUR

A Premature Post-Industrial Australia?

As noted in Chapter 1, no exploratory study of a post-industrial society can describe exactly what such a society is going to be like. However, one can say that the range of choice will be extremely wide, relative to industrial or pre-industrial society. Indeed, this is seen by many writers on the subject as one of the most important characteristics of a post-industrial society, even as a defining characteristic. Just how wide the range of choice will be is uncertain because any society must maintain a certain degree of unity, resilience, and tradition if it is to survive various challenges. This chapter makes an educated guess concerning the requirements for a post-industrial society, less to show what one might be like than to argue that such a society will probably not take shape in Australia until after the turn of the century — or even later if the country's economic and technological performance falls too much below its potential. This chapter is titled "A Premature Post-Industrial Australia?" to emphasize our belief that Australia might try to become post-industrial "too early".

The Concept of a Post-Industrial Society

A post-industrial society should be thought of largely as a reward for high performance industrialization. Such a society will probably emerge only very gradually, as the general level of affluence and technological capability permit a society to satisfy its basic priorities more easily; people can then move on to "higher" and hopefully "better" priorities, still within a given system of values. Eventually, people would become so accustomed to the new level of affluence and technology that it would be taken for granted and an altogether new set of values would become the norm. In a premature post-industrial society the values change too soon, leading to a mistaken re-ordering of priorities. For example, such a society is almost certain to expand support for the arts and other leisure activities — not because people have changed their values but because they would have plenty of money and time for these activities. In later generations, this change in priorities would bring about a change in values, less through exhortation or preaching than simply as a consequence of increased affluence. People would come to think of a new level of artistic and leisure activity as a matter of right. If they do so too early and too intensely, they might direct too many resources to these activities and not enough to more mundane, but still more essential ones. At any level of income and technology, a post-industrial society would give more support to cultural and artistic activities than an industrial society, but the eventual change in values would reflect a change in the nature of the people and the activities being pursued.

Such a transition would occur largely through declining marginal utility: at some point, the more one has of a particular good, the less one values the next additional unit of that good. When one is poor, a first car is extremely desirable and therefore very valuable. For many families, accustomed to driving everywhere, a second car is regarded as almost essential and therefore also very valuable. For families with teenage children, a third or even fourth car is often desirable enough to be worth its cost. But even for wealthy families who could afford still more cars, a sixth or seventh car becomes relatively less valuable than other goods such a family could buy with its plentiful resources. Even if the absolute cost of a sixth or seventh car is low, its relative value is so low that typically something else is purchased in its stead. Generalizing from this, as societies get richer, they gradually put less value on acquiring more of the goods they customarily produced in the past, and more value on producing and acquiring other goods and services.

As they have become more industrialized, societies have grown much richer: eventually they will probably become so sated with the amount of goods available that they will put less emphasis on acquiring new goods, and more on services and "leisure". The word "leisure" is in quotes because, as a post-industrial society develops more fully, the traditional distinction between work and leisure will probably become blurred and may even disappear. In terms of the concepts discussed in Chapter 2, the long-term consumption pattern for any good — and ultimately for the aggregate consumption of goods — approximates an S-shaped, or logistic, pattern more than an exponential one. Consumption does not continue to grow at an increasing pace indefinitely; it reaches a certain level and then more or less flattens out. While this process is not the only one operating, it determines much of what happens, particularly in a long-term context. (In the short term, many consumption patterns are affected by fads, status symbols, and other highly elastic factors; taken together, however, something like an S-shaped curve is likely to prevail over the long term.)

In this sense, economic growth is much like biological growth: it goes through several different and distinct stages, and eventually tapers off. However, the tapering off process will probably be more like that of a tree than a blade of grass. In other words, economic growth will not come to a complete stop, but rather reach a peak rate and then, assuming other things are more less equal, decelerate. A stable long-term growth rate might range from barely positive to barely negative, in contrast, say, to the 4.9 per cent average annual growth rate of the advanced capitalist nations (ACNs) during *La Deuxième Belle Epoque*. In qualitative terms, certain aspects of growth might die out and be replaced by new aspects. Individual societies could wax and wane, even in a world with more or less zero population growth.

As this process unfolds, mankind's pursuits could change radically. There are now more artists and accountants in the ACNs than in the early nineteenth century, and there are likely to be still more artists in the twenty-first century but far fewer accountants. Different societies and cultures will doubtless rise and fall. More dramatically, entirely new civilizations that represent a sharp break with earlier models might emerge. While this picture of the future emphasizes an ultimately much slower rate of economic change compared with the rate prevailing at the peak of the Great Transition, some change, even dramatic change, is still likely along with periods of great rigidity. The peak is the rate of change to the Great Transition is occurring during the present period, making it qualitatively different from every other period. This difference is manifested most clearly in the rapidity of technological change and the pace of increased affluence. Thus, barring an Armageddon, the world is unlikely to witness such extraordinary rates of change in the adoption of advanced technologies and increased affluence as have recently occurred. One might imagine an invasion from outer space, which forced the entire earth to mobilize totally in order to repel the invaders. This would presumably produce enormous investment and great technological progress in whatever fields were relevant to the mobilization effort — and greatly increased gross world product as well. But it is difficult to imagine any other event that would inspire an earth that had grown populous and rich to work at the kind of pace.

If the concept of declining marginal utility is applied to economic growth in general, then as different societies become affluent, they will cease at some point to be as economically dynamic as they had been. It is conceivable that a society might value dynamism for its own sake, and pursue economic growth as a kind of game — as a nice way to spend one's time. Or more plausibly, a society might pursue certain enormous projects — again, for their own sake or as a kind of religious activity. The goal of such a society might be to spread the human race to colonies on the moon or to other planets. A society might even make an enormous effort to reach the stars, and if so, it might well have high rates of growth for a very long time — roughly equivalent to the dynamism that was associated with the expansion of European power to other parts of the earth from the sixteenth through the nineteenth centuries. While no possibility can be ruled out, current trends seem, on balance, to be most plausibly described by the basic picture of an S-shaped curve, with societies reaching a peak rate of economic growth and then tapering off. At that point, post-industrial societies would have shifted their emphasis to other priorities, and subsequently to new values altogether. This process will doubtless be gradual; the change will be a matter of degree rather than kind. Australia, as one of the world's wealthiest countries to date, and one that is perhaps more willing than others to slacken off, may be among the first examples of this phenomenon. However, it is probably premature for any society, including Australia, to slow down its long-term growth rate deliberately and consciously, beyond the degree to which such a slowdown is occurring as a matter of course.

No society is yet in a position to justify slowing down on purpose. But the ACNs have reached a point where their goods are produced more efficiently than in the past: agriculture and manufacturing, for example, use considerably more capital and technology and considerably less labour, and thus are much more productive in terms of labour. Hence, the ACNs seem on the verge of becoming "post-industrial", able to achieve a certain (or even greater) level of output with a very small input of labour.

This kind of transition began to occur in agriculture in the mid-nineteenth century. Before then, most people had been engaged in subsistence agriculture. With the application of increasing amounts of capital and improved technology to agricultural production — in the form of seed selection, fertilizers, water control, improved farm machinery, irrigation systems, and genetic improvements — agricultural productivity and output began to increase enormously, and the amount of labour required to produce a given output began to decline. This provided a pool of labour that could be more efficiently employed in more complex activities such as mining and manufacturing.

Today, in countries like Australia, where large-scale agricultural production is highly efficient, fewer and fewer workers, as well as less land, are needed to produce an increasing volume of agricultural goods. (See Figure 4.1.) Indeed, countries like Australia and the U.S. feed themselves and other countries too. This concept of a "post-agricultural society" does not imply that agricultural output is unimportant — quite the contrary. Agriculture has become so productive precisely because so much

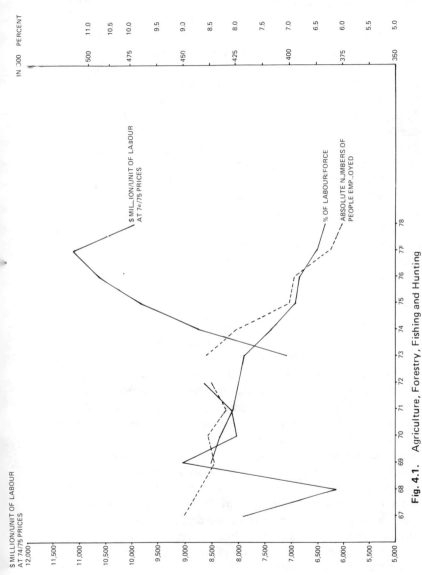

$ MILLION/UNIT OF LABOUR
AT 74/75 PRICES

$ MILLION/UNIT OF LABOUR
AT 74/75 PRICES

% OF LABOUR FORCE

ABSOLUTE NUMBERS OF
PEOPLE EMPLOYED

IN 000   PERCENT

Fig. 4.1. Agriculture, Forestry, Fishing and Hunting

Source: 1979 Yearbook of Labor Statistics, International Labor Office, Geneva.
Australian National Accounts 1977–78, Australian Bureau of Statistics, Canberra.

Note: break in series 1972.

care and attention were devoted to it. As output per unit of labour input increases, societies can devote a greater proportion of their human resources to non-agricultural pursuits.

A similar transition occurred more recently in mining. As Geoffrey Blainey notes, back in the 1860s Australian miners had to "climb down slippery vertical ladders to their working places and exhaust themselves at the end of the shift by climbing up hundreds of feet". After their arduous descent into the mine, "every miner used a heavy hammer to drive a sharpened rod of steel into the rock, turning the steel with his hand as the hammer struck".[1] Nowadays, safety standards and living arrangements are vastly improved, and production has been transformed by huge drag lines and power shovels which scoop iron ore or coal out of vast open-pit mines and deposit them into unit trains that go directly to port. The Australian mining industry produces some 4.5 per cent of total GDP with only 1.3 per cent of the labour force. (See Figure 4.2.) Here again, mining has not become less important to Australia: it has actually become more important as a proportion to GDP than at any time since 1920, but this has occurred without requiring a commensurate increase in labour.

In a post-industrial society, this same phenomenon would occur in manufacturing — and to some degree it has begun to occur already, although much less extensively than many have assumed. Indeed, current U.S. labour force and productivity patterns have not changed very much since the early decades of this century.[2] The eight hour day has remained a norm for fifty years, and despite liberal pensions and protracted schooling, a record high percentage of working-age Americans held jobs in 1978. Despite the expected rapid growth of government and other service jobs, manufacturing industries account for very nearly as large a proportion of jobs today as in 1925. This is frequently ignored or discounted. As in the 1920s, employment statistics are typically interpreted in the light of a conviction that the industrial era's dynamics of wealth and job creation are giving way to a new era. This is true, but the real question is at what pace. As was the case half a century ago, contemporary conventional wisdom still expects:

- the desire for more leisure to displace the desire for more income;

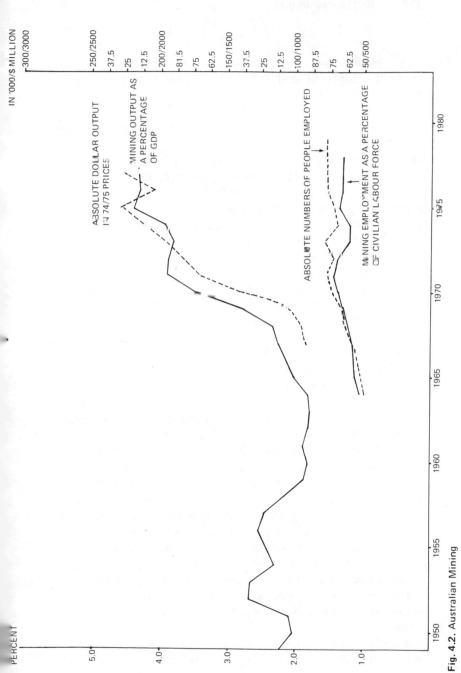

Fig. 4.2. Australian Mining

Source: Australian Bureau of Statistics, *Year Book Australia 1979*; and International Labor Office, *Yearbook of Labor Statistics*, various issues.

- goods-production to be a dwindling source of jobs;
- the less-educated to shift from blue-collar to service jobs;
- the public sector to experience fewer constraints on employment growth than the private sector; and
- additional growth-dampening effects from resource scarcities and pollution.

In each generation, this view has been sustained by evidence of changes in the expected direction, by an inability to imagine the future growth potential of demand for goods, and by a reinforcing set of value judgments. Thus, those who do the forecasting have generally assumed that affluence ought to breed more leisure and less interest in consumption, that service jobs are preferable to blue-collar jobs, and that more effort ought to go to needs that government serves.

Yet as high a proportion of male workers held manufacturing-industry (and construction-industry) jobs in the U.S. in 1973 as in 1950, and mining-industry jobs, while lower, were on the rise. If a major shift out of goods-production employment is emerging for men, this is a new, not a long-term, trend. The important job trends for men have been out of farming, and from lower to higher skill levels *within* the white and blue-collar sectors. The apparent reduction of the workweek for wage and salary workers has been almost entirely a function of the growth of the female workforce in jobs that had shorter than average hours. (Only a slight change for men exists, even if adjustment is made for public and annual holidays.) Since this trend was not accompanied by a proportionate decline in the time women spend on unpaid housework, the sum of "free time" since 1958 may be viewed as declining rather than rising, thereby strengthening the argument that Americans have continued to show a marked preference for increased purchasing power over increased leisure. Such data suggest that the role of "persistencies" in the work system has consistently been understated and underprojected. By implication, current analyses of prospects for work and leisure may also be systematically underestimating the obstacles to "expected" trends.

Data for Australia follow a similar pattern. Figures 4.1 and 4.3 show that while labour attrition from agriculture has been steady

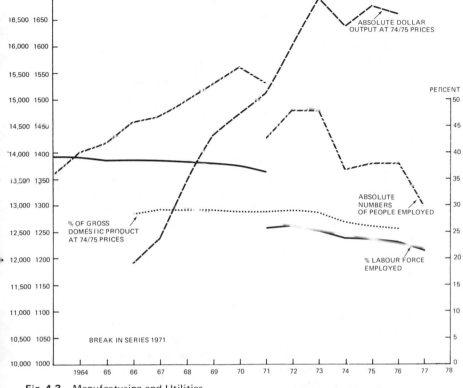

Fig. 4.3 Manufacturing and Utilities

Source: 1979 Yearbook of Labor Statistics, International Labor Office, Geneva.
        Australian National Accounts 1977–78, Australian Bureau of Statistics, Canberra.

Note: break in series 1971.

for more than a decade, manufacturing as a percentage of the labour force declined only slowly until the recession of the mid-1970s. This suggests that manufacturing may experience a slight recovery, or even a gain, after it has adjusted to increased costs. The manufacturing sector has also declined only slowly as a percentage of GDP.

Despite the caution suggested by such data, we believe that trends in Australia and other ACNs will eventually move in a post-industrial direction. In the language of utility theory, at some point the value of the next unit of gain in manufacturing can be expected to decline relative to the previous unit. As in agriculture and mining, fewer people would be needed to manufacture a given level of output — again, not because manufacturing becomes unimportant or unnecessary, but because it becomes more productive through increased capitalization and improved technology. Such productivity gains in the industrial sector set the stage for increases in the size and scope of services.

In terms of the traditional classification system used by Colin Clark and Simon Kuznets,[3] an economy can be divided into a primary sector (agriculture, forestry, and mining), a secondary sector (manufacturing) and a tertiary sector (services). As Clark and Kuznets noticed, when economic growth began to accelerate, the primary sector began to decline as a percentage of total output and as a percentage of the labour force. Correspondingly, the secondary and tertiary sectors began to increase. Nowadays, in Australia and most other developed countries, the secondary sector has also reached a plateau, as a percentage of both total output and the labour force, though the details vary from country to country. (See Figure 4.3.) By implication, the tertiary sector will probably grow further to take up the slack. (See Figure 4.4.)

To date, the tertiary sector has grown more or less predictably, but future trends may proceed somewhat differently from a "straight-line" projection of previous changes. For one thing, although the percentage of the labour force employed in the primary and secondary sectors has declined, the rate of decline has probably already peaked, meaning that the decline itself is tapering off evermore gradually. In theory, a point might be reached where hardly anyone was employed in the primary and secondary sectors; robots and computers would replace almost all humans. In actuality, the decline will probably never reach this point, though it might get remarkably close. Most of the human activity that remained might be more white-collar than blue-collar: more like the tertiary sector in terms of occupation area, even if the job were officially classified as being in the primary or secondary sector. Moreover, the tertiary sector is no longer dominated by low productivity work; instead it is characterized by an ever-changing

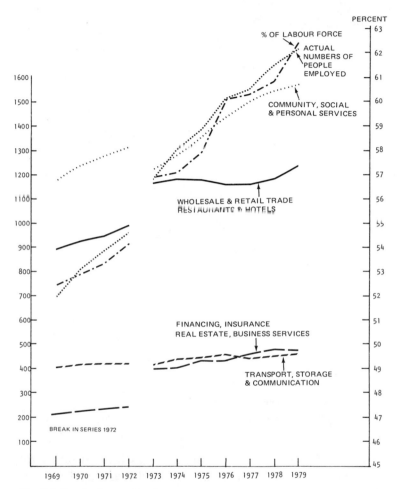

PERCENT

% OF LABOUR FORCE

ACTUAL NUMBERS OF PEOPLE EMPLOYED

COMMUNITY, SOCIAL & PERSONAL SERVICES

WHOLESALE & RETAIL TRADE RESTAURANTS & HOTELS

FINANCING, INSURANCE REAL ESTATE, BUSINESS SERVICES

TRANSPORT, STORAGE & COMMUNICATION

BREAK IN SERIES 1972

Fig. 4.4. Service Sector Employment

Source: 1979 Yearbook of Labor Statistics, International Labor Office, Geneva (1979 extrapolations: Hudson Institute).

Note: Break in series 1972.

combination of low and high productivity work, with the latter increasingly important as growth proceeds. This has come about for two reasons: initially, high-productivity work stemmed mainly from the human capital (that is, education) invested in people in the service sector; more recently, the productivity of individual

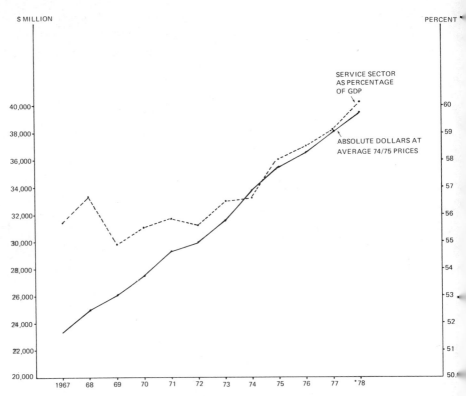

Fig. 4.5. Service Sector as Percentage of GDP

Source: Australian National Accounts 1977—78, Australian Bureau of Statistics.

workers with a given level of education has been increased by computers, other modern technology, and managerial innovations.

Previous Hudson Institute studies carried the traditional three sector categorization a step further, and distinguished between a tertiary sector, defined as services oriented toward the primary and secondary sectors and toward itself (that is, oriented directly or indirectly toward the production of goods), and a quaternary sector, defined as services done for their own sake or for the direct satisfaction of consumers.[4] The idea was to distinguish between services that were needed to support other sectors of the economy and those that were directly valuable in their own right or as a way station to other activities valuable in their own right (such as physical training for sports, education for self-actualization, and religious activities).

However, even this four-sector categorization seems inadequate. To reflect the forces actually at work, a further distinction is needed in the tertiary and quaternary sectors between activities that can be automated or whose productivity can be otherwise greatly increased, and activities whose productivity cannot be automated or greatly improved upon. For simplicity, the sub-sectors can be thought of as "automatable" and "non-automatable".

The time available to an individual is one aspect of economic life that cannot be expanded — there are still only twenty-four hours in a day. Hence, any activity that uses a person's time but cannot be improved upon through capital or technology will become increasingly expensive. In pre-industrial societies, many activities in the service sector were actually personal services or their equivalent. The cost of an individual's time was typically lower than the cost of whatever machinery or equipment was available; as a result, work was usually labour-intensive, and wealthy people could readily employ large staffs. As per capita output began to rise precipitously, first in the primary and subsequently in the secondary sector, the relative prices of goods and services began to be reversed. Aided by capitalization and technology, goods became cheap and services became expensive — at least those services in the tertiary and quaternary sectors which could not be automated.

This is roughly the situation facing any developed country today. Since there can be no significant increase in the productivity of these services, and since the potential demand for them does not diminish — most people would still enjoy having a chauffeur — the cost of the service becomes the limiting factor. Moreover, there can be no foreseeable concept of declining marginal utility in these sectors — a chauffeur would continue to be desirable for some time. Again, of course, values may follow priorities — after people have not had chauffeurs for some time, they may eventually not want them, even if they suddenly become available. For most ACNs, a majority of people are now no longer employed in the primary or secondary sectors; in a post-industrial society, this would also be true for the automated part of tertiary sector. People would then be employed largely in the tertiary sub-sector which could not be automated, and which would remain relatively labour-intensive (teachers, for example), and in the quaternary sub-sectors (televised adult education teachers and poets). The exact mixture among these sub-sectors will depend on the skill, taste, and ingenuity of different people. Moreover, for many quaternary activities, the distinction between work and leisure will lose much of its earlier meaning.

In fact, there is already no sub-sector which can be considered purely "non-automatable". Take the example of religion: an activity pursued for its own sake, usually not for profit and not considered a business. However, with the advent of televised religious ceremonies, a preacher's sermon can reach a great many more people (even if, as some say, the quality of the product is diminished). The extra jobs that this gain in productivity generates (television crews, advertising for religious books, authors for these books) clearly become an economic as well as a religious activity. This gain in productivity from televising religion also creates the possibility of more jobs which cannot be automated as more people may enter the field of religion (there are probably more Billy Grahams today than ten years ago, which of course implies a sharp distinction between them and the traditional preachers). Another example is the televising of education, which would lead to more jobs not only for the technicians required to broadcast classes but also for teachers, at least if the need for classroom teachers itself continues.

This sub-sector categorization is a modification of ideas developed by William J. Baumol and William G. Bowen, who argued that since the productivity of services was unlikely to increase as much as productivity in the primary and secondary sectors, the potential growth of services would be more limited than that of other sectors. In a detailed description of the economics of the performing arts, they argued that no amount of automation or other capital or technological improvements could alleviate a string quartet's need to practice a certain number of hours and to play a certain composition for a certain length of time. Hence, they said, string quartets and other work with similar characteristics would become increasingly expensive.[5]

Baumol and Bowen are correct regarding services that cannot be automated, but they failed to notice that modern technology could considerably automate or otherwise improve many service activities such as banking, insurance, and fast-food restaurants. In the case of string quartets, their audience also as been greatly expanded through capitilization and technology; new developments in audio equipment have enabled string quartets to pick up much more revenue than an audience for a single live performance might provide. Thus, they have increased their earning power enormously.

Some might argue that the difference between a live performance by a string quartet and a recording is so great that string quartets should basically be classified as non-automatable, but most people would be just as willing to consider them automatable precisely because their productivity has been enormously increased. Certainly owners of stereo equipment or car cassette players would think of string quartets as capable of automation; this group is surely more numerous than those who would deign to listen only to live performances.

A post-industrial society will share many socio-economic characteristics with a pre-industrial society. Before industrialization, many people might have been officially classified in the primary or even secondary sectors, when in fact they spent only part of the year working in these sectors, at harvest time for example, and the rest of the year in some kind of service or simply under-employed, which is a more or less disguised form of leisure. A similar phenomenon can be expected in a post-industrial society in that people might be employed for only part of the year, or for much shorter hours and/or with much longer holiday periods. People might work up to a certain income and spend the rest of their time in leisure or in some other pursuit they would take very seriously — typically a quaternary activity which was not automated and which they would enjoy doing and might even operate for a profit, but would not think of as a business or as their occupation. However, to a statistician from Mars, making a first visit to earth, the pre-industrial and post-industrial forms of under-employment would have many similarities; if such a statistician were from a rising industrial society with high morale and enough young people to support large military forces, the post-industrial version of under-employment might look decadent and the society ripe for conquest. The big difference between services in pre- and post-industrial societies lies in the value of the labour that goes into them. Where capital and technology cannot supplement or substitute for a certain minimal level of human effort, any service requiring this high degree of effort is likely to become enormously expensive.

But from the viewpoint of the average person, the deprivation caused by the high cost of services which cannot be automated is much less than the benefits derived from the relatively low cost of services which can be automated. Deprivation becomes as much a problem for the rich, or the upper middle class, as for the rest of society. A rich person who is interested in music can "indulge" himself by buying high quality records and playing them on high quality audio equipment. Such a person might even derive a lot of satisfaction from marginal differences in the quality of the recording or the audio equipment he has purchased. But he might just as easily feel deprived, since, unlike his forebears, he cannot afford a live performance in his own home; he might even feel deprived because the quality of his audio equipment is not vastly superior to that available on the mass market. On the other hand, the average person who buys an ordinary record and plays it on normal equipment is not particularly concerned that live performances in one's home have become prohibitively expensive. They are out of his reach in any case; moreover, the difference between a live performance and an average record is, to him, not so great — in some ways the recording may even be preferable since it can be played at the listener's convenience. The rich person who insisted on a live performance would get something extra for his money, but probably not very much extra.[6] Meanwhile, the average person is likely to feel that he gets a lot out of a record collection and a stereo set.

This distinction between services is vital to understanding many current issues as well as future economic development, particularly for a relatively isolated society like Australia, which might take a long time to recover from a diversion onto an unproductive path. For example, many Australian workers feel the computer is more a threat than a benefit, since it can so obviously improve the productivity of services, and thus eliminate many jobs The computer seems especially well-suited to highly standardized services like banking, insurance, government record-keeping, and certain kinds of management services. However, in normal circumstances, services in the tertiary and quaternary sub-sectors which can be automated can be easily expanded. Experience in many countries and the history of technical innovation suggest that although the computer and other communications technology will cause some dislocation in the labour market, the degree of dislocation (after adjustments) would be no more than would normally be expected from any change in the conditions prevailing in a market economy. In such an economy, things are always in flux — or should be — which is what makes market economies more efficient than other types of economies.

One can also expect that the number of people engaged in running computers will probably exceed the number engaged in the earlier, pre-computer activities that have been computerized. An innovation produces a demand for new kinds of services. There may even be a certain amount of "make work" in these new services, but they nonetheless exist and are supported by the system. Thus, if an office establishes procedures to photocopy various documents (an activity that did not exist until recently), there is a tendency to make a large number of copies, some of which may be processed, stored, or sent to many people simply as incidental information. Whether the extra number of copies and the expense entailed in handling them are always worthwhile is perhaps an open question, but it is a new activity that requires much effort and people to provide the effort. More importantly, the computer allows all kinds of specialized information to be gathered, processed, and reproduced in a form that would have been prohibitively expensive before the advent of the computer. And when this new information does become available, the demand for it goes up enormously. An example might be information on accounts, which in modern banks is now available not only at one's own branch but throughout the system — a distinct advantage to the customer (and to the bank, and presumably to society in general), and a new activity that also requires people to operate it. And here, too, values follow priorities — people who look at a cathode ray tube only when they have to will eventually be replaced by a younger generation that prefers getting information from a CRT to getting it from a book.

In the long run, of course, services follow the path of primary and secondary activities, that is, fewer people are needed to provide the required output, and the marginal utility of increased activity in these services probably also declines; in any case the number of people involved will almost certainly decline. Over the very long term, only services with unlimited demand are in the non-automatable sectors, and relative to this demand, the supply seems almost certain to decline. Hence, relative to automatable services and to goods in the primary and secondary sectors, services which cannot be automated will be relatively scarce; their price will be relatively high, and many will not be available. The hardship entailed also has a tendency to decrease as values follow priorities, so that, after not being able to get live-in servants, people tend eventually not to desire them.

As these trends unfold, a kind of backlash against the use of personal services might even develop. At an extreme, people might prefer to be their own psychoanalyst, lawyer, teacher, entertainer, and so on. Even in this case, however, demand for non-automated services would continue at some level. The main issue in the interim may be society's ability to adjust rapidly to technological change as it affects the sectors which can be improved by automation. Technology's ability to increase the productivity and output of these sectors should exert a great influence on economic dynamism. As long as new automatable services can be expanded and/or shift to the non-automatable subsectors, then increases in the productivity of older automatable services should not lead to an increase in aggregate unemployment. The new services create completely new opportunities for leisure, for new services, and for the transfer of jobs to non-automatable sectors in the same way that improvements in the primary and secondary sectors lead to increased opportunities for new manufactured products, services, and leisure.

Adjustment problems for some parts of the labour force will certainly arise, particularly among older and less educated employees who are not easily retrained. But it is very much in the interest of most workers to adopt whatever degree of computer-ization or other technological innovations that can be incorp-orated into the tertiary sector. As affluence and public welfare increase, the issue from the individual's viewpoint is whether the available jobs will be sufficiently remunerative and attractive to be worth taking, rather than whether there will be enough jobs in the aggregate. In many developed countries, standards of accepta-ble remuneration and attractiveness have risen more rapidly than the number of new jobs. More precisely, if the level of unem-ployment benefits is not that much lower than a regular salary, many people prefer the dole to a job that falls below their aspira-tions. People want jobs commensurate with their abilities and expectations. To the degree that they can work only in those terti-ary or quaternary sub-sectors which cannot be automated, their expectations might price them out of the market. If these same people could work in the automated sub-sectors, they would nor-mally enjoy the dignity that goes with high-quality service jobs, but not be too expensive to employ.

Thus, the term post-industrial society is used here in a techni-cal sense — it is a society capable of producing a large output of primary and secondary goods with a relatively small input of labour. Thus services become relatively expensive unless they can be made more productive through the increased use of capital or advanced technology. Some services which cannot be auto-mated may become less available, either because people will be unwilling to pay high prices for "low-priced" work (for example maids) or because people will be unwilling to work in jobs they consider undignified.

This accounts for much of the anger felt about growth by peo-ple in the upper middle class. In a highly developed society, where non-automated services have become very expensive (and consequently less easily consumed), the upper middle class feels "cheated"; it fails to get what it thought was its due, and sometimes feels so cheated that it cannot understand that economic development is still a goal for the middle class and below.

A Premature Post-Industrial Society

Many people who live in developed countries may assume they are already living in a post-industrial society, even though all the pre-conditions for such a society do not yet exist. Indeed, various versions of a premature post-industrial society can be found in Australia.

One version stems from the notion that a society has already achieved a level of affluence sufficient for the rest of history — that it is already rich enough to need no additional wealth. This attitude is found almost exclusively in ACNs. It first cropped up in the mid to late 1960s, loosely linked to a host of other manifestations of the counter-culture. Although this view is seldom explicitly stated, it is expressed in lifestyles and in positions taken on particular issues of the day, such as protection of the environment at virtually any cost, including future development. Younger people tend to hold these views more intensely than their elders. As the hippie slogan of a few years ago put it, the time had come to "turn on, tune in, and drop out". In effect, history was thought to have stopped — or to be about to stop once the "errors" of the Vietnam war were rectified by an American (and concurrently an Australian) withdrawal. There would be no more famines, no further need for national defence, no further invasions or rebellions (except those that were "justified"), and so on. This version of a premature post-industrial society was particularly prevalent among upper middle class adolescents who have led a very sheltered life — which in fact resembled life in a post-industrial society. Hence the concept that the world has already become post-industrial came to them all too easily. Because their experience has been so limited, it was hard for these adolescents to understand that they behaviour of most people everywhere is sill governed by the need to earn a living — and that this need would come to them too.

To some extent this vision of a post-industrial society is correct; as societies become richer, they can afford to put less emphasis on survival, defence, health, avoiding famine, and so on. But if societies reach the point of not worrying about these problems at all, and take affluence and safety for granted, they will virtually invite some kind of catastrophe. Thus, it is important to realize that a post-industrial society needs to be defined more clearly, that it is likely to come into being only slowly and gradually, and that even then the "Four Horsemen of the Apocalypse" (famine, pestilence, invasion, and revolution) will not automatically be eliminated from the earth.[7]

The idea that Australia is already rich enough — if not for the rest of history, at least enough to allow most people to slacken off or for the development of a "no hassle" society — is not uncommon among residents of the suburban areas of the five state capitals. Living on an isolated continent, and enjoying a temperate climate and easy access to boating, tennis, golf, and similar recreational facilities, many suburban Australians think that they already possess everything they would ever need. They realize that not everyone living in the state capitals are affluent, but many are much better off than they were in the past, and this affluence is much more equally distributed than in the U.S., for instance; furthermore, racial tensions, crime, and pollution are relatively unobtrusive. Hence, it is easy to imagine that someone living in one of these state capitals or in Canberra might feel not only that things are just fine as they are, but also that nothing should be done to upset the status quo.

Another example of premature post-industrialism is a society that has been evolving in that direction but has failed to reach its objective. It becomes an "arrested industrial society", inadvertently stabilizing at a relatively low level of wealth. This can come about in many ways. Uruguay is probably the best example, though contemporary Britain is a more widely known case of arrested development. Uruguay adopted an excessive orientation toward welfare early in the twentieth century, before it had become wealthy enough to support this policy. As a result, Uruguay has been unable to attain anything like the potential it was once thought to have. Argentina is a similar example, though its disappointing record has been cushioned by a highly productive agricultural sector. In Britain, excessive demands by trade unionists in recent years have clearly deterred investment, even though the fall of the pound in the mid-1970s should have encouraged considerable new investment there.

These cases are relevant to contemporary Australia. For example, the Australian government could tax the country's resources to the point of taking business for granted and thereby impeding its development; this actually happened during Prime Minister Whitlam's tenure. Although some forms of a resource tax might not harm the resource sector and might even enhance the productivity of Australian society as a whole, other forms might — and did — scare off potential investors. With regard to labour disputes, if Australian society had developed a genuine consensus that workers were entitled to engage in wildcat strikes, there would be less reason to question this practice. The freedom to engage in such strikes would then just be part of the Australian standard of living. However, if these strikes interfere too much or if Australians were bitterly divided over such practices, the resulting societal tensions could easily slow economic development prematurely.

While many societies are probably heading in a post-industrial direction, this outcome is not inevitable. Also, the pace at which this evolution occurs is almost as important as the basic trend itself. Those who aim for a post-industrial society but overestimate the real level of wealth risk bringing about certain aspects of such a society prematurely — thus endangering or delaying the emergence of a true post-industrial society. The trend toward a post-industrial society should be natural and inevitable, a result of actual productivity increases. But what is a natural pace? This raises the familiar problem of trying to establish distinct categories within a continuum. It is relatively easy to draw such distinctions qualitatively and roughly, but much more difficult to do so precisely and quantitatively.

In the mid-1960s, for example, Kahn suggested that a post-industrial society would probably begin to emerge when average income reached about $4,000 (in 1965 U.S. dollars).[8] This is roughly equivalent to $10,000 in 1980 U.S. dollars, or about where U.S. per capita income is today. Although few would say that the U.S. has no post-industrial aspects, even fewer would argue that it has already become a fully post-industrial society. While such a society is clearly emerging, it is not doing so very rapidly, in part because certain influential elites are acting as if it had already emerged. The difference between an emerging and a fully post-industrial society is much greater than seemed evident fifteen years ago, and the transition is clearly much more difficult to accomplish. This change in emphasis reinforces our feeling that no country is wealthy enough as yet to be regarded as more than a slowly emerging post-industrial society.

Nevertheless, qualitative changes can be illuminating. For example, when an Australian secretary complains that her overseas trip was spoiled because she ran into so many other secretaries there, she is expressing a concern that was once associated only with the rich. Such phenomena indicate that a society is adopting upper middle class, if not upper class, attitudes. In other words, an emerging post-industrial society is characterized not only by a relative decline in manufacturing and in services which lend themselves to automation, but also by changes in certain attitudes. Suppose, for example, that a country is deeply concerned about its manufacturing sector, even though only 5 per cent of the labour force is employed in that sector; as a result a lot of attention is paid to manufacturing, and public policy consciously tries to strengthen it. Such a society would not be fully post-industrial, because it would be overly concerned with industrial activities. Such activities in a post-industrial society can be compared to the task of ensuring that a modern city has potable water: it can normally be left to technical experts. Doing so competently is not particularly difficult, but those responsible must maintain professional standards, pay attention to details, look for new innovations, and in general take nothing for granted. However, they need not be as vigilant and dedicated as their counterparts in a developing country. In an advanced society, potable water is seldom an emotional or political issue. However, if this vital service were taken for granted or neglected, serious difficulties could easily arise.

To summarize, the prospect of a post-industrial society should not be confused with its arrival. Once an industrial society reaches maturity, certain tendencies begin to operate which either push it too quickly toward a seemingly post-industrial status or erroneously suggest that this status has already been achieved. A country like Australia, which, like any ACN, can be described as an emerging post-industrial society, faces a choice: it can decide either to make a premature post-industrial society even more premature, or, alternatively, to slow the pace at which post-industrial policies might be adopted and seek instead to become more fully post-industrial over a longer period of time.

Quality of Life Shift

Many different paths to a post-industrial future can be imagined, varying according to the level of wealth, from a society that tapers off at $50,000 to $100,000 per capita income to a society that tapers off between $10,000 and $20,000 per capita. Societies may also vary according to such qualitative differences as their level of welfare and leisure-orientation, or the degree to which they might pursue big projects such as commercially viable supersonic aircraft, space travel, or, perhaps in Australia's case, the successful achievement of a much dreamed of "watering of the desert". A prototype for this particular project already exists in the American southwest, where infrastructure developments over a period of a hundred years now yield such benefits that a whole new — and primarily urban — society has been created on once arid land. This transformation has been accomplished largely through increased applications of technology, which have not only made residential living in such hot climates feasible, but have gone so far as to create artificial seas in otherwise desert climates.[9] The great difference between an industrial society undertaking such grandiose projects and a post-industrial society doing so is that the latter can afford to pursue such goals as a matter of relatively free choice — that is, it is not forced into such projects in order to survive, but can choose among a whole range of projects, or opt instead for more welfare, more leisure, and so forth.

Before industrialization, mankind's activities were limited either by the requirements of survival, or by relatively strict requirements of the productive system. People were tied to the land by the necessity of remaining close to the source of food. Areas of high population density simply did not exist because supplies of food could support only limited numbers of people. Industrialization expanded these limits. Areas of greatly increased population could then be supported, partly because increased agricultural productivity enabled people to work in non-agricultural jobs, which in turn generated new productivity increases. Meanwhile, improved transportation systems enabled people to move greater distances than had been possible in pre-industrial days. Gradually, people became tied not to the land but to the factory, the place and means of industrial production. In contemporary times, this tie has been loosened by further improvements in transportation; thus it is not uncommon for people to reside more than fifty kilometres from their place of work.

Having a wider range of choices, people quickly widen their range of desires: the familiar spiral of increasing expectations. Nowadays, there is little reason to expect a farmer's son or daughter to stay on the farm, especially in view of the changes in farming already discussed. Goods on display in big cities raise and spread the expectations of the general population still further, at least initially. Later on, the demand for material goods will taper off along the lines suggested by the S-shaped curve.

This concept of a wider range of choice is particularly applicable to changes in the United States during the past ten years, notably in helping to explain large internal migrations from the colder northwest and midwest to warmer climates in the southeast and southwest. Although this phenomenon is sometimes labelled a "sunbelt shift", it is referred to here by the broader term, a "quality of life shift". The reason is that much the same criteria seem to have motivated people to move to colder areas such as western Massachusetts, Colorado, and Oregon, as well as to the warmer climes of the south. Although the lure of sunshine cannot be dismissed, the common element in the movement to these booming localities has been the attraction of a certain lifestyle. From the U.S. experience one could argue that, as any country gets richer, it will also see large internal migrations based on a search for high quality of life in a new location. However, a number of specifically American characteristics have made these population shifts especially strong there. Among these are the precedent set by an earlier population shift to California and the relatively high social mobility of the U.S. population (in part because of extensive changes in the social structure wrought by World War II and in part because of continued infusions of new immigrants that help keep the society mobile).

In Australia these factors have been less compelling. Australians are already settled — overwhelmingly so — in the most climatically desirable parts of the country; indeed, very few Australians live anywhere else. Hence, the conditions for a large-scale movement from a "snowbelt" to a "sunbelt" do not exist.

Nonetheless, as noted in Chapter 3, there has been a slight outward movement from the more populous states towards Queensland and Western Australia. An acceleration of this trend in the 1980s would not be surprising. Businesses might find it advantageous to set up new facilities on the west coast, slightly north or south of Perth, along lines advocated for many years by Sir Charles Court. Similar developments might take hold on the northeastern coast of Queensland, where towns have been settled for more than a hundred years and, relative to the west coast, a physical and social infrastructure is already in place. Even New South Wales, though older than other states, is not yet so settled as to preclude further in-migration in search of lifestyles based on an attractive climate and a varied economy.

In all of these cases, the precedent of the American southwest may be applicable. In Arizona, sampling data suggest that lifestyle considerations were the major motivation behind the 40 per cent

Table 4.1. The Trend in Lifestyle Indicators — Metropolitan Phoenix

	1969	1977	Percent Change
Population	966,000	1,360,000	41%
Employment	383,200	493,000	29
Number of College Students	52,915	89,619	69
Number of Boats (State Wide)	40,081	80,806	102
Shopping Center Area (In Millions of Square Feet)	13.1	26.1	99
Number of Shopping Centers	127	210	65
Households with a Second (Vacation) Home in Arizona	8,000	19,000	138
Households with Factory Air Conditioned Automobiles	57%	79%	38
Households with a Swimming Pool	8%	14%	75
Percent of Retired Households under 65 Years of Age	23%	29%	26
Percent of Households Swimming in Past 30 Days	31%	45%	45

Source: Paul Bracken, *Arizona Tomorrow: A Precursor of Post-Industrial America*; (forthcoming).

increase in population that has occurred there since the late 1960s, and various indicators illustrate the prevalence of a modern, affluent lifestyle.[10] A shift from a primarily goods-producing to a primarily services-producing economy and a key technological breakthrough — the spread of central air conditioning — were important spurs to growth (See Table 4.1 and Figures 4.6 and 4.7.). Some shift within the goods-producing industries has occurred toward so-called "clean factories", in which, for example, high value-added steps in a manufacturing process are undertaken in an electronics plant in Arizona, while lower value-added steps are undertaken in South Korea, with the unfinished goods air-freighted back and forth between the two workplaces. Something like this, with probably an even stronger export orientation than would be necessary for a U.S. manufacturer, is conceivable for manufacturing in Australia, either in the already populated southeastern states or at new manufacturing sites in the so-far less populated states of Queensland and Western Australia.

People have typically sought to take advantage of the benefits that affluence and technology provide in the form of new choices. This has been less true, however, during the past decade, when various upper middle class groups have discouraged the development of new areas in order to preserve the natural environment,

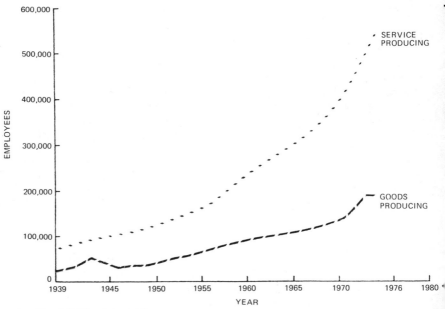

Fig. 4.6. The Arizona Economy

Source: Paul Bracken, *Arizona Tomorrow: A Precursor of Post-Industrial America*; (forthcoming).

or simply to maintain the status quo because they are against further growth anywhere. That this has happened is no reason to accept it as inevitable. Public policies can be designed to prevent anti-growth attitudes from carrying a disproportionate weight — or at least to ensure that such policies are understood to involve choices between growth and the status quo.

What does this discussion of a post-industrial society mean for the future of Australia? To summarize the argument, a post-industrial society would be capable of producing an abundance of goods and services with a minimum amount of labour; it would thus be a society productive enough and wealthy enough to afford

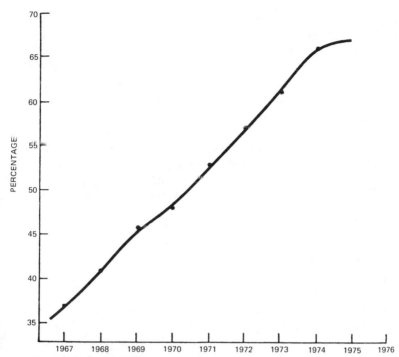

Fig. 4.7. Air Conditioning in the Desert. Percent of metropolitan Phoenix homes with entire house air conditioned

Source: "Crime and the Future of Arizona," by Paul Bracken, 1979. Data developed from information provided by Arizona Public Service, Inc., and Salt River Project, Inc., Phoenix.

an abundance of welfare or leisure — or the luxury of pursuing almost any goal. No country, including Australia, is yet in a position to consider itself fully post-industrial, and for this reason Australia should avoid making the mistake of assuming that the benefits of a post-industrial society already exist for the taking. Such mistakes are most likely, of course, if society or its leaders reach for such benefits prematurely.

Australians can hinder or facilitate the attainment of a post-industrial society in various ways. The most effective way to facilitate this process is to exploit the growth potential of advanced technology, not only in agriculture, mining and manu-

facturing, but also in services. The main method by which an affluent society remains productive is to promote those services that
are most amenable to automation. To oversimplify, the situation
can be described as a choice between welcoming computerization
as a boon that will create new jobs (which it almost certainly is) or
opposing computerization as a menace to the security and com-
fort of contemporary Australian lifestyles.

With a vast and bountiful continent at their disposal, Australians have few reasons to oppose growth or to hinder the introduction of new technology. Such an attitude amounts to defeat-
ism on a grand scale. The troubles of contemporary Britain show
what can happen to a country that assumes it is post-industrial
prematurely, by emphasizing consumption at the expense of
investment or by trying to preserve the status quo in an ever-
changing world. If Australians want the rewards of a post-
industrial society, they will have to work for them, and continue
working to maintain them. Productivity increases over time are
the path to a post-industrial future, but such increases also have
to be maintained after a post-industrial stage has been reached. In
other words, people will live in a post-industrial garden only if
they make the effort to keep it weeded. The weeding can be made
much easier through modern technology — one may not have to
bend over to dig out the weeds, and chemical pesticides can prevent some weeds from taking root — but the garden cannot be
neglected altogether. At the same time, new developments in
technology make all sorts of possibilities feasible. For example,
the Australian outback need not be arid forever: in time, vast
stretches of now-empty land will almost certainly be settled,
especially by a wealthy, productive society as rich as a post-
industrial Australia.

The requirements for maintaining a post-industrial society do
not seem too onerous; they are certainly less onerous than maintaining a pre-industrial or industrial society. And the prospect of a
post-industrial future is alluring enough to inspire sober thought
and hard work. Though a full-fledged post-industrial society may
still be many years in the making, such a vision is needed to provide Australians a goal that is both feasible and rewarding.

Notes

1. Geoffrey Blainey. *The Rush that Never Ended*, 3rd ed. (Melbourne: Melbourne University Press, 1978), pp. 77-78.
2. This and the following paragraph draw on material developed by Jane Newitt. See *Why Do We Have So Many Jobs?*, Hudson Institute Corporate Environment Program, Research Memorandum No. 51 (Croton-on-Hudson, N.Y.: May 1978).
3. See, for example, Colin Clark, *The Conditions of Economic Progress*, 3rd ed. (New York: St Martin's Press, 1957), and Simon Kuznets, *Modern Economic Growth: Rate, Structure, and Spread* (New Haven: Yale University Press, 1966).
4. See, in particular, Herman Kahn, William Brown and Leon Martel, *The Next 200 Years* (New York: William Morrow and Company, 1976) and Herman Kahn, *World Economic Development* (Boulder, Colo.: Westview Press, 1979).
5. William J. Baumol and William G. Bowen, *Performing Arts — The Economic Dilemma* (New York: The Twentieth Century Fund, 1966), especially pp. 161-172. Baumol and Bowen went on to argue that this "iron law" of services constituted a powerful argument for government support of the arts, the idea being that private individuals could no longer afford string quartets and society as a whole would gain from their being preserved.
6. A night out with, say, Zsa Zsa Gabor is probably still preferable to a disco-vision of her. And there is always some benefit to snob value. But in general, the "deprivation" to society as a whole from the loss of the night-with-Zsa-Zsa-style services is probably bearable.
7. Indeed, our colleague Max Singer has suggested that they may be joined by four more "horsemen" who, in this context, may be even more dangerous: affluence, apparent safety, hedonism, and self-indulgence.
8. See Herman Kahn and Anthony J. Weiner, *The Year 2000* (New York: The Macmillan Company, 1967), chapter III.
9. See Paul Bracken, *Arizona Tomorrow: A Precursor of Post-Industrial America* (forthcoming), and a summary, "Arizona: Precursor of Post-Industrial America", in *The Futurist*, Vol. XIV, No. 1, February 1980, pp. 35-48.
10. Ibid.

FIVE

A Revitalized Australia?

Previous chapters have described a business-as-usual future as the most likely alternative for Australia, at least for the ensuing ten to twenty years, and a post-industrial future as the eventual goal toward which all ACNs are heading. However, some countries might mistakenly think they have already reached this goal, and adopt certain post-industrial policies without having achieved the wealth or productivity gains to justify such policies. More accurately, certain classes in these societies, particularly the upper-middle class, may move towards these policies and attitudes, while the rest of society acquiesces. This chapter looks at the opposite side of this coin; it describes various policies that Australia, as well as other developed countries, might follow to advance expeditiously and relatively painlessly toward a post-industrial society. There are different ways of looking at the problems of an emerging post-industrial society that became particularly evident in the 1960s and 1970s and that, in turn, strengthened the tendency of all ACNs to think of themselves as prematurely post-industrial.

In lieu of a business-as-usual or a premature post-industrial future, Australians might choose either a reformed protectionist or an economically dynamic future. Both would require surmounting those Australian attitudes that reinforce economic pressures for a business-as-usual alternative, or those tendencies in any ACN that tempt a country to adopt a premature post-industrial alternative. A program of reformed protectionism would involve a number of relatively small changes designed to make the economy operate more efficiently. The steps in such a

program would include a gradual reduction, both in the protectionist trade barriers that have traditionally sheltered the Australian economy, and also in various other policies that have closely
regulated the economy. In a reformed protectionist future,
some Australians would give up some of their current standard of
living for the sake of a higher standard in the future. An economically dynamic alternative would introduce an even greater degree
of change, particularly in long-term goals; it would build upon (or
modify) those steps taken in a reformed protectionist future and,
more importantly, would seek to carry such steps much further.

Australia, like other ACNs, has resisted making the kinds of
changes involved in these two alternatives because such changes
mean that, while some people gain, others lose. In democratic
societies recently, prospective losers have been able to form
interest groups to fight creative destruction much more easily
than potential winners have been able (or willing) to get together
to lobby for such changes. In terms of the New Emphases mentioned in Table 2.1, this resistance to changes goes beyond the
"natural and inevitable" and becomes unreasonable and obstruc-
tive.

Both reformed protectionism and economic dynamism require
short-term changes in order to realize long-term benefits. Both
are feasible only if a strong leader or a consciously mobilized
population can bring an extraordinary degree of effort to bear on
the problem. These are obviously difficult conditions to meet.
Even Japan, whose record in making structural adjustments has
been better than other ACNs, was more intent on change during
the fifties and sixties than in the seventies. As societies grow
wealthier and more comfortable, they often come to feel that the
extra effort required for change is no longer as important as it
once was. Thus, during the 1970s, Japan became less sure of
where it needed to go, or even of where it wanted to go — at least
until it began to feel challenged by middle-income countries like
South Korea and Taiwan.

Australia is also being challenged by the middle-income countries. At the same time, a combination of current conditions and
attitudes seems to have created an unusual consensus that something should be done to make the Australian economy operate

more efficiently. Recent government-commissioned studies have
pushed for less protection, as have almost all of Australia's economists and social critics who have written on the issue.[1] Sections
of both management and labour have issued strikingly similar
pleas for increased productivity, and warnings about the dangers
of relying too much on Australia's resource endowment.

The major political parties, though naturally attuned to short-
term interests, are under pressure to shift away from traditionally
partisan lines toward a more centrist approach. While, a centrist
trend could strengthen feelings of complacency, it could also, if
coupled with a conscious attempt to revitalize the Australian
economy, provide strong support for any growth-oriented program. In addition, the mini-boom conditions that have developed
in Australia during the past eighteen months — notably the
much-increased interest of domestic and foreign investors in
Australia's coal, natural gas, shale, and uranium — give the
country a tremendous opportunity to use the increased capital
inflow generated by these projects to improve the productivity of
all sectors of the economy. Indeed, the country must now try
consciously to improve the efficiency of the non-resource sectors, simply to ease those upward pressures on the Australian dollar which have been generated by increased investment in
resources.

Under current circumstances, both in Australia and other
ACNs, the difficulty is that many proposals for structural adjustment seem harmful not only in the short-term sense in which all
change is disruptive, but even in some ways from a long-term
viewpoint. A major country needs some degree of manufacturing
in order to feel "complete" — to maintain a broad-based technological capability and a mobilization base in the event of an
external military or economic threat. The problem is to decide
where to draw the line between reasonable and unreasonable subsidies for these purposes.

Manufacturing

Previous attempts to bring about a reformed protectionist program have emphasized inefficiencies in parts of Australia's

manufacturing sector. Manufacturing is often assumed to be the main source of employment in Australia — or at least the main solution to recent problems of high unemployment. Resistance to change is also greatest in this sector, partly because of the desire to keep a manufacturing sector for national security reasons and partly because of tradition or habit. The focus of economic growth in almost all ACNs has been on manufacturing for so long that further declines are often seen as much more alarming than those that have occurred to date. Hence, interest groups that seek to defend the status quo in the manufacturing sector are the best organized and the most readily supported opponents of creative destruction. The result, especially in recent years, has been a stalemate. The Australian manufacturing sector has declined, both as a percentage of GDP and of the labour force. The more important trend for the future, however, is that parts of the manufacturing sector — notably motor vehicles, white goods, and textiles, clothing, and footwear — have become much less competitive. Consequently, such sub-sectors are much more in need of subsidies — or change.

But harping on the inefficiencies in the manufacturing sector is likely to yield little more than a continued knocking of heads with interest groups that have the power to block or greatly delay changes in this sector. The issue is almost always looked at from a negative viewpoint, with discussions focusing on what jobs will be lost rather than on what jobs might be gained. This is understandable, since no one knows exactly what will result from structural change, only what should result if the market economy mechanisms are operating according to theory. No one can prove that a more competitive atmosphere in the Australian economy will generate the necessary degree of entrepreneurial behaviour to counteract the losses entailed in opening the economy to more imports. Thus, as an approach to policy making, an emphasis on either the short-term losses from structural change or the longer-term losses from a failure to adjust is too negative to promote effective action: it offers little assurance to those who stand to lose, and does nothing to mobilize support for structural change among those individuals or interest groups who stand to gain.

Any effective program of structural change will require both car-

rots and sticks. The fears of increased unemployment associated
with possible further declines in the manufacturing sector would
be greatly alleviated if more persuasive arguments could be used
to show why increased productivity in any part of the economy
almost always leads to increased employment rather than a loss of
jobs, at least in the aggregate. Economic growth has always made
some jobs obsolete, but it has always created new jobs also.

There is much to be gained by emphasizing the growth potential — in both productivity and jobs — of the service sector. The
future growth of most ACNs is likely to come from increased
specialization in *both* manufacturing and services, and to this
extent any program of reformed protectionism or economic
dynamism is likely to be more effective if it emphasizes the car-
rots — the positive gains to be made in an increasingly productive
service sector — than if it continues to emphasize the sticks —
the so far unheeded warnings of future stagnation stemming
from a relatively static manufacturing sector.

Continued pressure on the manufacturing sector will promote
those adjustments which will eventually mean greater efficiency
in the sector to the advantage of the Australian economy as a
whole. This is why earlier studies have recommended a reduction
in tariffs and a shift toward a more specialized manufacturing sector. If this process were to unfold, Australia would import a wider
range and a greater volume than before but it would also export a
greater volume than before, either high technology finished products (such as dry-farming machinery) or relatively high technology or skilled labour-intensive components (such as parts of a
new "world car").

There are numerous ways in which the operation of the
manufacturing sector (and the economy as a whole) could be
made more productive — each worth a study in themselves, and
each important, if not essential, elements of any thorough-going
program of reformed protectionism or economic dynamism.
These would include:

1. a continued emphasis on controlling inflation;
2. liberalization of capital markets;
3. de-regulation of domestic transport, particularly coastal ship-
    ping and airlines;
4. stronger efforts to link wage increases to productivity gains;

5. greater consistency and reliability in raw material development policies, where long lead times and export markets
   make these attributes especially important to potential investors.

All of these issues have long been identified as areas in which, if
action were taken, the Australian economy would operate far
more efficiently.

To cite one example, coastal shipping laws have made it 44 per
cent more expensive to transport steel from Port Kembla on the
east coast to Fremantle on the west coast than from Japan to
Fremantle.[2] Looking at the same point from a different angle,
the Industries Assistance Commission estimated that the Broken
Hill Proprietary Company, Australia's main steel producer,
spends between $20 and $25 million a year more to transport iron
and coal around the coast in Australian ships than it would cost
using those sailing under foreign flags of convenience.[3] Since
every benefit has a cost, one commentary looked at these numbers and posed the question of whether this degree of protection,
which it valued at $15,000 to $19,000 per person per year to keep
thirteen hundred seamen employed in the B.H.P. fleet (which
accounts for roughly half of Australia's entire coastal fleet),
might not be better spent some other way.[4]

The technical problems involved in resolving such issues as
these, while certainly formidable, would be manageable if the
motivation to act were there. And to the extent that Australia's
manufacturing sector can become more productive by realizing
any of these reforms, or perhaps through greater sales to fast-
growing markets in the Asia-Pacific region, any such improvements would constitute an unqualified gain to the economy as a
whole. But even if made in full, these improvements could never
provide the main solution to Australia's economic problems. In
all ACNs, the service sector is becoming increasingly significant,
both as a source of employment and output, and even more
importantly as a source of productivity growth. Manufacturing will
remain essential to any advanced country, but in an emerging
post-industrial economy, its share of GDP — though not its
absolute size — will almost certainly decline. And, like
agriculture and mining, the manufacturing sector will neither

need nor receive the kind of attention it still gets in economic discussions in most ACNS.

Services

The service sector — the tertiary and quaternary sectors together — has for some time been much larger than the manufacturing sector, in terms of both output and employment, in the economies of most ACNs.[5] In Australia's case, it is two-and-one-half times larger than manufacturing as a percentage of GDP and almost three times larger as a percentage of the labour force. In absolute terms, it is more than twice as large in terms of output and one-fourth larger in total people employed. (See Figures 4.3 and 4.4.)[6] Traditionally, economists have regarded services as a slow-growing sector. As a result, growth in the share of services has usually been viewed as a drag on the economy. Moreover, even though the service sector includes such "sober" pursuits as banking and teaching, there has been a general tendency to regard manufacturing as more "essential" to the overall economy. It has often been assumed that as economies mature and services expand, the more restricted potential for productivity growth in services would limit the growth of the economy as a whole.

Recent trends suggest that this traditional view is no longer valid, and recent research suggests that services may be on the verge of a productivity explosion.[7] If so, services could well become the leading sector, in terms of productivity growth, in the economies of the ACNs. This possibility is sufficiently real in Australia for both the facts and their policy implications to be investigated and evaluated as a matter of priority.

Measurement of productivity in the service sector has long been recognized as a much more difficult process than in the other sectors, where output is usually more tangible and more easily measured. In many cases, the value of the output of a service has simply been measured by the cost of inputs, or, as with the services of government, simply by the value of labour inputs. With the increased use of technology and highly educated workers in service sector jobs, this method is becoming increasingly inadequate. As a measurement of the productivity growth of government services, it implies that a bigger bureaucracy is more productive than a smaller one.

If improved methods of measuring producitivity in services could be agreed upon, the results of the application of new technological and managerial innovations would become more evident. In the meantime, developments in computer technology, particularly the micro processor, are likely to cause a considerable improvement in future productivity trends in the service sector. Recent developments in office automation, data processing, medical diagnostic equipment, telecommunications, and fast-food chains are probably only the beginning of a continuing application of new technological and managerial techniques to services. Services can become far more productive in terms of labour inputs, if and as they incorporate such innovations.

The growth potential of services, like that of agriculture, mining, and manufacturing, depends on productivity growth. In an emerging post-industrial society (where the potential range of services becomes more varied and the potential demand for new services is so great), the ability of an economy to develop highly productive services will have a decisive influence on its overall growth potential. Hence, policies that encourage investment for modernization and productivity increases should be emphasized. An increase in investment, such as the installation of a computer, may lead to a short-term reduction in employment, but it is more likely to increase productivity or create new possibilities so much that it stimulates new levels of demand, for that same service or for new services, in either case creating new jobs. Thus, the conditions for continued growth are basically the same for manufacturing and for services; flexibility is essential for the optimal allocation of resources. But the service sector, being (in its present form) newer and more varied than the other sectors, has many fewer vested interests, and correspondingly fewer people or groups bent on preserving the status quo. Hence it is, and is likely to remain, much more responsive to pressures for structural change than the manufacturing sector.

It has been remarked how the seemingly fixed productivity of a string quartet (or other such entertainers) has been increased enormously by the development of records and audio equipment. Recorded music has greatly increased the size of the listening audience, and improvements in the quality of recorded sound have increased the demand for both recorded music and live performances. At the same time, the recording of a live concert has enabled the producer (and the performers) to make a profit even with lower costs of admission. Instead of live concerts becoming prohibitively expensive, the application of modern technology and marketing has made possible more live performances as well as high sales of recorded music.

Barber shops are an example of the flexibility and speed that service businesses frequently display in response to new trends or fashions. Rising affluence brings changes in lifestyles, and men no longer feel uncomfortable when they patronize services that until recently were aimed exclusively at women. But the time required to cut a man's hair is more or less fixed; no amount of machinery can help a barber perform this service in less than fifteen minutes, at least according to commonly accepted social standards. (Army haircuts, which are performed in perhaps two minutes, are not normally considered commonly acceptable or commercially viable.) This limitation means that the price of a haircut is determined largely by the prevailing wage for semi-skilled work. To raise wages or profits, barbers have changed the nature of their service. They have added more value to their work, not by installing new technology but by adding capital to create, in effect, a new product, the man's hairstyle, in contrast to a mere haircut. The hairstyle often includes such "essentials" as protein shampoos, pretty girls to walk around the shop, facials for men, and so on. In this way, the shop is providing the customer with a bit of pizzazz, which has its own price tag.

These and other services listed in Table 5.1, have recently shown high economic growth in the United States. To the degree that American and Australian societies are similar and follow trends prevalent in most ACNs, these same businesses can be expected to grow in Australia as Australian per capita income continues to grow.[8]

Australia obviously has much to gain both from the further development of its vast untapped natural resources, and from

Table 5.1. Some Services with Recent High Growth in the U.S.

Adult education	Discos	Needlepoint shops
Air conditioning repair	Domestic services	Nursing homes
Airlines	Electronic funds transfer	Oilfield services
Amusement parks	Electronic mail	Package delivery
Automobile repair	Environmental monitoring and control services	Participant sports
Automobile telephone	Fast foods	Party planners
Banking	Fertility and natality-related services	Plant shops (indoor)
Cable TV	Gambling	Private security services
Car washes	Game stores	Religious centres
Catering	Gardening and landscaping establishments	Restaurants
Ceramic shops	Health clubs	Services for pets
Cheque clearing	Health food stores	Special education
Computer stores	Hospital supplies and equipment	Spectator sports
Conference centres	Hotels	Sporting goods
Consumer financial advisory services	Lawn services	Telecommunications
Convenience grocery stores	Legal services	Transportation equipment
Dance studios	Live theatre	Travel services
Dating services	Men's hairstyling	Vacation home swapping and rental
Data processing	Moped stores	Wine production and distribution
Day care	Movies	Wood processing
		Yoga, karate, TM, etc.

Source: This list is adapted from material developed by Irving Leveson. See "The U.S. Economy: Old or New," in *World, Regional, and National Trends and Issues*, Report of a Joint Conference by the Hudson Institute Corporate Environment Program and Hudson Research Europe World 1995 Program (Croton-on-Hudson, N.Y.: April 1979).

whatever revitalization of the manufacturing sector is feasible. But like other ACNs, Australia has been shifting to services for many years, for this is "where the action is". This shift can be expected to continue, if only because new services, based upon ever-more specialized tasks, can easily be created when supported by productivity increases.

Recent Australian economic comment recognizes the potential importance of the service sector, but is laden with fears that labour-saving innovations cause chronic unemployment.[9] The Crawford Committee concluded that "there are significant areas of the service sector that will not provide new job opportunities at the same rate as in the past".[10] This is true but there is at least as strong a case that other, equally significant areas of the service sector will provide new job opportunities to make up for — and probably more than make up for — those jobs that are lost. By failing even to address this possibility, the Crawford Committee gives the impression — without actually saying so — that technological innovations are detrimental to the economy.

If Australian society continues to regard such innovations as the computer with suspicion then the service sector will very likely become much more costly and less productive. But if the computer and similar technological innovations are welcomed and flexibility encouraged by the labour force, then adjustments almost certainly will be made, and the outcome could well be an increase in the aggregate number of jobs — and, more importantly, an increase in the kinds of jobs that most people want.

The issue of jobs is a central reason to emphasize the service sector, but not because of the scarcity of jobs. Rather, the issue is to create suitable jobs — that people are qualified for, and will accept. Once a society becomes affluent enough to provide for large-scale subsidies to the unemployed, the system becomes susceptible to a more subtle form of abuse than the traditional kind of "dole bludging". People who feel entitled to unemployment benefits when available jobs fail to satisfy their expectations may be considered voluntarily unemployed. With a relatively high level of unemployment benefits and a relatively easy procedure for obtaining them, Australia is probably more affected by this phenomenon than most ACNs.[11]

An earlier Hudson Institute study speculated that a leisure-oriented society in the year 2000 might see a work year of less than twelve hundred hours, which is about twenty-four hours per week. (See Table 5.1.) In an emerging post-industrial society, a shorter working week will become increasingly evident — and feasible. Already the service sector is attracting people, particu-

Table 5.2. A Leisure-Oriented Society (∿1110 working hours per year)

     7.5 hour working day
     4   working days per week
     39   working weeks per year
     10   public holidays
     3   day weekends
     13   weeks per year holidays
     (or 147 working days and 218 days off per year)

Thus, in such a leisure-oriented society, one could spend:

     40   per cent of one's days on a vocation
     40   per cent of one's days on an avocation
     20   per cent (or more than 1 day per week) on neither —
          that is, just relaxing

In an affluent, leisure-oriented society, of those (40 per cent) normally in the labour force:

     50   per cent work a normal year
     20   per cent moonlight
     10   per cent "half-time hobbyists"
     5   per cent frictional unemployment
     5   per cent semifrictional unemployment
     5   per cent revolutionary or passive "dropout"
     5   per cent "voluntarily" unemployed
     ___
     100 per cent

Source: Adapted from Herman Kahn and Anthony J. Wiener, *The Year 2000* (New York: The Macmillan Company, 1967), pp. 195-96.

Note: This pattern is characterized as leisure-oriented, rather than post-industrial (as it was described in the earlier book), to emphasize how an economy can be leisure-oriented without achieving the high productivity that is necessary for a truly post-industrial society. To adopt aspects of a leisure-oriented society without the accompanying high productivity is, of course, a value judgment that different individuals might choose to make or not make. To choose this course is at the very least premature.

larly women, who prefer to work part-time or on an irregular
schedule. This flexibility is also a plus for the employer, who is
relieved of otherwise rigid (and higher) labour costs. Such flexibility is also both a cause and an effect of less unionization in the
service sector. But the trend need not destroy or decisively
weaken trade unions if they adjust to new conditions as flexibly as
the employees and employers.

In principle, there is no difference between services and other
sectors of the economy either in terms of their contribution to
GDP or in their receptivity to productivity growth. In practice,
productivity growth in the manufacturing sector has become
unusually dependent on social and political attitudes, as well as on
economic factors. But the service sector is more open to change,
and is likely to become even more productive through the application of new technological and managerial innovations. In terms
of social and political forces, it is less rigid than other sectors; it
has fewer unions, fewer lobbyists, and fewer entrenched interests
generally. As ACNs become more affluent, their service sectors
will tend of their own accord to become more important.
Australia must decide how productive both its manufacturing and
service sectors will become, given its own past and the performance of other countries.

Investment

If productivity is to increase in any sector of the economy, there
must first be increased investment. Normally, significant
increases in investment only occur in the expectation of increased
demand. But in the conditions of persistent stagflation that have
recently characterized almost all ACNs, Keynesian methods of
stimulating aggregate demand cannot be used for fear of aggra-
vating inflation still further. As a result, economists have become
increasingly attracted to so-called "supply-oriented economics".
The idea is that only by creating or increasing productivity growth
on the supply side of the economy can the high rates of inflation
that have prevailed since 1973 be reduced; with greater productivity, an increased (or less costly) supply of goods would become

available to meet a relatively stable level of demand (which would be kept stable by tighter control of the money supply).

This emphasis on supply-oriented economics is probably still in its early stages, reflecting a still growing recognition that the problems of *L'Epoque de Malaise* are different from those of either a *Belle Epoque* or a *Mauvaise Epoque,* and thus require different solutions. Many details must still be worked out, but basically the role of government in a dynamic capitalist economy would shift from one of correcting inequities in the distribution of wealth to one of correcting newly-arisen barriers to the production of wealth. At this point in the development of the ACNs, such a shift is altogether reasonable.

All ACNs are, in varying degrees, emerging post-industrial societies. Unlike the developing countries, which have the model of the already developed countries to follow, the ACNs themselves have only the vaguest idea of where to go from here. As discussed in Chapter 4, one can imagine a genuinely post-industrial society as one in which agriculture, mining, and manufacturing would all be extremely productive, in terms of labour inputs. Parts of the service sector would become similarly productive, while other parts would either have to become extremely expensive or to be thought of as leisure activities. But the progression from a pre-industrial to an industrial, a super-industrial, and then a post-industrial society, however likely, is still neither easily envisioned nor inevitable. To the degree that affluent societies are tempted to give too much emphasis to consumption and protection of the status quo, they do so at the expense of productivity, investment, and creative destruction. The malaise currently afflicting the ACNs suggests that, wittingly or unwittingly, they are in danger of succumbing to this temptation, and thus of adopting post-industrial values prematurely. It is therefore logical for the role of government to counter-balance the otherwise natural tendencies in society, which in current circumstances means a government policy shift toward the role of trying to promote productive efficiency. This does not mean the government should try to stop the progression to a post-industrial society or even slow it down in an overall sense. Rather, the government should facilitate this progression, which paradoxically means it may need to slow down parts of the trend that, in themselves, have gotten too far ahead of the rest of society.

As discussed earlier, various social and institutional changes that accompanied increased affluence led to a series of fiscal, monetary, and regulatory policies that contributed to an extended build-up of inflationary forces. In many ways, a rising rate of inflation can be regarded as a rough index of the degree to which a society is living beyond its means. In the ACNs, where people have known good times longer than in any other group of countries, such "built-in" inflationary pressures have been accumulating for a longer period of time, and are correspondingly stronger. Among the ACNs, the Atlantic-Protestant countries have the longest record of peace and prosperity (in part due to less war damage than incurred by most other ACNs). They also have the longest record of democracy. Thus, the willingness of some groups in these countries to take the benefits of economic growth for granted becomes a much stronger force than it otherwise might because of the ability of such special interest groups to command attention. This is not to argue against democracy, but simply to recognize some of its consequences.

Inflation may well be the most difficult problem for an affluent democratic nation to solve — more difficult even than an external challenge. The economic, social, and political consequences of chronic inflation are all extremely serious. Chronic inflation greatly discourages capital investment, as well as eroding the value of assets, encouraging excessive borrowing, and in the absence of bracketed indexation bringing about unlegislated tax increases. These consequences lead, in turn, to such corrosive social effects as the use of expense accounts as a supplementary source of income and the growth of "underground" economies. Chronic inflation also exaggerates the normal inequities of society by making the issue of who gains and who loses in a business transaction even less predictable. Any market economy includes a necessary degree of uncertainty; in an inflationary environment, these uncertainties are magnified by the likelihood that one would either over-anticipate or under-anticipate the degree of inflation. For a while at least, people may imagine that indexing will prevent or minimize such distortions and keep the system stable, but again, the longer the inflation persists, the greater the amount of formal or informal indexing sets in, and the more the economy becomes prone to an explosive inflation — and then to a potentially even more explosive reaction.

To prevent things from building up to such an extent, governments may have to allow or even induce recessions. Difficult though it may be to accept, recessions of some sort are necessary from time to time to eliminate moderate rates of inflation and head off the even greater pain that would be caused by high and/or chronic inflation and are inevitable in a capitalist economic system even in the absence of inflation. Recessions are easiest to bear if they are short and shallow, rather than having to become, after a prolonged period of inflation, long and deep. The constant use of stimulants to postpone periods of mild recession or to stimulate recovery only makes the eventual collapse that much greater, and the recovery from such a collapse that much more difficult.

Mustering the discipline needed to allow for frequent, small downturns in the business cycle is difficult enough; once inflation rates have begun to fall it is even more difficult to refrain from letting up too soon. Just as governments — particularly democratic governments — have sought to postpone recessions through Keynesian stimulation, they are similarly tempted to ease up on tight monetary and fiscal policies in order to improve short-term employment prospects. But the long-term trade-off remains. Many have argued that unemployment in an affluent society is immoral or at least intolerable. We would argue, however, that inflation is at least as immoral or intolerable since it causes arbitrary transfers of wealth, from creditors to borrowers and from citizens to governments. In fact, since a much larger proportion of the population is adversely affected by inflation than by unemployment, a majority might feel that inflation is more immoral or intolerable. Besides, in conditions of stagflation, continued inflation actually worsens unemployment, and, to the degree that chronic inflation risks a severe depression, it worsens long-term employment prospects much more than anti-inflation policies worsen employment prospects in the short-term.

Because the current inflation creates distortions throughout the economy, anti-inflation policies are easily the most important steps that Australia, or any ACN, could take to improve prospects for investment and thereby revitalize its economy. Many other measures could also be taken, of course, depending on how extensive a revitalization Australians want — and how much they are willing to sacrifice. We have distinguished, for example, between a "reformed" protectionist and economically dynamic alternatives. In both cases, various policies might be introduced not only to lower the rate of inflation, but also to create positive incentives for increased investment. In the case of economic dynamism, such incentives would seek to promote the most efficient forms of investment regardless of what sector of the economy they occurred in. In "reformed" protectionism, these incentives would probably be biased in favour of the manufacturing sector, either because Australians felt (in our view mistakenly) that manufacturing were a better source of employment than other sectors, or because Australians felt more secure and more "complete" as a nation by having a wider range of manufacturing industries than would be dictated by strictly free market criteria.

We mentioned earlier, in the context of the manufacturing sector, various ways in which both manufacturing and the economy as a whole might be made more productive. Any of these measures — a liberalization of capital markets, de-regulation of domestic transport, etc. — would also increase incentives to invest. The economy would still be subject to cyclical ups and downs, but in a structural sense, this increased investment would lead to greater efficiency and almost certainly to higher average growth rates.

Depending, again, on how vigorously Australians wanted to promote investment, they might wish to re-open consideration of a value-added tax. To the degree that income taxes have already begun to reach a point of diminishing returns, some new forms of taxation will have to be considered. But a value-added tax has the advantage of taxing consumption, and thus of indirectly encouraging saving and investment. It has the additional advantage, under current trading rules, of being rebatable on exported products — in other words, a value-added tax does not raise export prices. On the other hand, value-added taxes do require large bookkeeping efforts, though with computerization this burden can be lightened considerably. Traditionally, economists considered value added taxes to be "regressive", meaning that a greater burden from the tax would fall on the poor than on the well-to-do; for example, in the case of a consumption tax, the poor consume a greater proportion of their income and thus suffer a greater loss. But value-added taxes are levied in more than half of the OECD countries, and evidence from their experience, though brief, suggests that its regressive character has been over-estimated, and indeed can be offset by setting higher tax rates on higher-quality goods.[12]

A resource rent tax is another frequently mentioned source of government revenue, and, in turn, of potential productivity increases. The idea is that Australia's natural wealth belongs to the public as a whole, and should therefore be taxed for the benefit of everyone. In fact, as the downturn in resource development during the 1970s showed, the real problem is not one of how to "squeeze" a maximum amount of tax from a bountiful supply of resources; rather, it is one of trying to prevent a resource tax from becoming so confiscatory that it deters investment and development. Indeed, the more bountiful the particular resource in question, and/or the cheaper it is to obtain from competing sources of supply, the less leeway there is to levy a higher resource rent tax. Erratic policies toward resource development can also have — and in Australia in the 1970s did have — an extremely negative effect on resource development. Again, if one had to choose, we would argue that Australia would do better to err on the side of lower, rather than higher resource rent taxes. The public for whose benefit a resource tax is intended actually benefits more from a steady and growing resource sector with a relatively small tax rate than from a smaller or declining resource sector with a relatively high tax rate.

For any revitalization program, the investment that is required to achieve productivity increases has to cost something. There is no "free lunch", even in Australia. With a growing economy, however, the choices that must be made are rather less stark than in a static economy — and they boil down to a choice between how much to consume in the short term versus how much to invest for the long term.

The Idea of Progress

The traditional concept of progress, as defined in Western culture, has been under attack for more than a decade, though less so in recent years as counter-arguments have asserted themselves. In any case, the 1974-75 recession caused many people to see once again the value of economic growth. Meanwhile, during this same period of self-doubt in the West, the countries of East and Southeast Asia have achieved such unprecedentedly high growth rates that they can now be said to embrace the idea of progress, as previously conceived in the West, more enthusiastically than is currently the case in most Western countries. Many who worry that economic growth in the ACNs has slowed too soon, or too much, argue that this stems from the very success of the growth process itself. As Mancur Olson puts it:

> . . . democratic countries with freedom of organization gradually accumulate powerful common-interest organizations with monopoly power or political clout, and . . . these organizations (though they have some favourable effects, too) are likely to lower the rate of economic growth. . .[13]

Thus, in Australia, as in most ACNs, vested interests in the manufacturing sector have resisted the very structural changes made necessary by past success. This resistance has been bolstered by a similar, if not greater, reluctance on the part of trade unions to permit corresponding adjustments. The result, for both management and labour, has been steady decline in competitiveness, masked until now by protectionist measures made increasingly expensive as other countries become more developed.

The solution, to the extent that one is visible at all, lies in directing the focus of attention to productivity increases in all sectors of the economy, particularly in the service sector. This means a reaffirmation of the idea that market forces are the best method of assuring the efficient allocation of society's resources. As a by-product — a critically important by-product in an epoch of malaise — the efficiency of the market will be far more effective than the political process in dealing with special interest groups of any kind. An Australian economy that seeks efficiency also need not fear competition from abroad — whether in the form of imported goods, imported capital, or immigrants. It could make use of all these assets to complement and supplement domestic resources, and in the process give the economy further strength and confidence.

Notes

1. Many of the recommendations made by these observers have been ignored or shunted aside, but this does not mean the consensus is not stronger than before
2. John Barber, "The Growth Potential of the Australian Steel Industry", in Wolfgang Kasper and Thomas G. Parry, eds., *Growth, Trade and Structural Change in an Open Australian Economy* (Kensington, N.S.W.: Centre for Applied Economic Research, University of N.S.W., 1978), p. 301.
3. Industries Assistance Commission, *Draft Report on Iron and Steel Industry* Part A, *Basic Iron and Steel Products* (Canberra: Commonwealth Government Printer, 1979), p. 94.
4. Bank of New South Wales, "A New Direction for Australian Manufacturing?", *Review* 29 (June 1979): p. 9.
5. See Angus Maddison, "Economic Growth and Structural Change in Advanced Capitalist Countries", in Irving Leveson and Jimmy W. Wheeler, eds., *Western Economies in Transition: Structural Change and Adjustment Policies in Industrial Countries* (Boulder, Colo.: Westview Press, 1980), pp. 47 and 51.
6. Data cited by Maddison and data cited in Figures 4.3 and 4.4 are not strictly comparable.
7. See in particular, Irving Leveson, *The Modern Service Sector,* Hudson Institute Corporate Environment Program, Research Memorandum No. 83 (Croton-on-Hudson, N.Y.: January 1980), and "Productivity in Services: Issues for Analysis", paper presented at the Conference on Productivity Research of the American Productivity Center, Houston, Texas, April 1980; see also Maddison, "Economic Growth and Structural Change in Advanced Capitalist Countries", and Maurice Lengelle, "The Development of the Service Sector in OECD Countries and Its Implications for the Economy of the Western World", in Leveson and Wheeler, *Western Economies in Transition,* and Maddison, "Long Run Dynamics of Productivity Growth", *Banca Nationale, del Lavoro Quarterly Review,* 128 (March 1979): pp. 3-44.
8. For description of similar trends in Japan, see Kazuo Nukazawa, *The Implications of Japan's Emerging Service Economy,* Keidanren Papers, 8 (Tokyo: Federation of Economic Organizations, 1980), especially pp. 25-27.
9. See, for example, the statement of the Department of Employment and Industrial Relations, in the report of the *Study Group on Structural Adjustment* (Canberra: AGPS, 1979), pp. 5.5-5.6.
10. Ibid., p. 12.
11. Australia is one of the few countries in the world where a person can receive unemployment benefits without having worked previously and/or paid into

an unemployment insurance system. To some extent, a policy that permits school-leavers to go directly on holidays at government expense is simply another consequence of increased affluence. Yet it is hard to imagine a worse policy than making unemployment benefits easily available to indifferently motivated young people who have never had a job and then having them abuse the privilege. While the number of such people is small, the example is known all over Australia. Clearly, if this were to increase greatly, society's ability to support such a system would be strained, financially and morally. Alternatively, any emerging post-industrial society that sought to maintain such a system would quickly become prematurely post-industrial.

12. See OECD, *Public Expenditure Trends,* Studies on Resource Allocation, No. 5 (Paris: OECD, June 1978), p. 76.

13. Mancur Olson, "The Political Economy of Comparative Growth Rates." in U.S. Congress, Joint Economic Committee, *U.S. Economic Growth from 1976 to 1986: Prospects, Problems, and Patterns,* Volume 2, (Washington: U.S. Government Printing Office, 1976), p. 25.

SIX

Australia and the World

This study of the future of Australia began by asking whether Australia is a model of what lies ahead for the rest of the world. The answer is both yes and no. Australia, as one of the wealthiest of the developed countries, has already begun to face questions that are likely to confront all countries as they become comparably developed: how much time to spend working, how much on leisure; how much value to put on consumption, how much on investment; how well should a country live in the near-to-medium term, how carefully should it look out for the medium-to-long term; how quickly should a society seek to become post-industrial, and in what way; how might it slow down, or speed up, this process? Australia has begun to face these questions sooner than other countries, and is in this respect a model for others; to the extent that it has not yet answered these questions, Australia can only provide a model or likely problems, not of the most desirable solutions.

Australia's answers to these questions are not yet known: a business-as-usual future seems most likely, at least for the rest of this century, but a premature post-industrial Australia, or reformed protectionism or economic dynamism, are all plausible, possible choices as well. This range of choice at least is open to Australia, including a mixture among these alternatives.

As countries become more affluent, their range of choice expands. The world's poorest societies can do little more than stay where they are, or mobilize for economic growth. The middle-income countries, having begun to grow, typically try hard to maintain high growth rates. Only when societies have become reasonably affluent can they afford the luxury of choosing how much further they wish to grow and in what way. Australia, like other ACNs, has begun to feel the effects of the New Emphases, to prefer stability to growth, and to think of creative destruction as more destructive than creative. In this sense it is a microcosm of how any advanced capitalist nation might face the question of what path it should take in the future. All ACNs will encounter both the continuing problems of adjustment and the continuing opportunities for growth associated with the development of middle-income countries.

Australia and Asia

Australia is a special case. Because it is relatively isolated, it is protected more than other ACNs from some of the short-term changes taking place elsewhere in the world, but at the same time is more exposed to the long-term effects of these changes. As a sparsely populated, predominantly European-settled society near a densely populated Asia, it faces substantially different problems from other predominantly European or European-settled nations. Australia's problems in adjusting to the growth of nearby middle-income countries with a different racial and cultural makeup are likely to appear more visible than the otherwise similar adjustment problems of most other ACNs, though because the growth prospects of the Asia-Pacific region ar so favourable, the potential benefits to Australia are also likely to be more visible — and perhaps greater.

The pros and cons of continued economic growth for the ACNs have been discussed in largely economic terms. Yet one benefit of increased wealth has traditionally been an enhanced capability for national security. If one could easily analyze such factors, they might well indicate that national security, rather than economic welfare *per se,* has been the main motivation for economic growth. In most ACNs, the results of earlier economic growth are now a legacy of the past, and taken all too much for granted. The traditional relationship between economic growth and national security has become much less obvious in most

ACNs than it is, even now, in Japan, and certainly less obvious than in the fast-growing middle-income countries of Asia, including, of late, China. Thus, in addition to whatever "purely" economic factors might make Australians forego a certain degree of consumption for the sake of a greater degree of investment, the near-certainty that various countries of Asia will be doing this is a compelling reason for Australians to consider their future rate of economic growth in the context of their security vis-à-vis other countries in the Asia-Pacific region.

The issue is much more subtle than clear-cut. None of the four likely futures for Australia over the next ten to twenty years represents a sharp break with current trends. But in the context of the continuing high growth rates that Asian countries are likely to achieve during this period, the choice that Australia makes among these four alternatives might significantly affect the choices open to the country in the twenty-first century. Even then, the situation facing Australia may still be more subtle than clear-cut. Although provision must be made for further uncertainty in the international political environment, stemming from a further decline in American political and military power, the U.S. is likely to recover some of its lost ground in the early to mid-1980s, if only because the Soviet Union may also encounter domestic difficulties, either from a succession crisis, economic strains, or both. The effectiveness of American power in the past — and its continued effectiveness in spite of recent difficulties — would continue to shield Australia from the starkest external threats that a small country might face. Thus, for the 1980s, and perhaps the rest of the century, Australia's main problems will probably be more internal than external.

Even with regard to internal problems, the situation is likely to be more subtle than clear-cut. Although a business-as-usual future would lead to a gradually less competitive country, and one that is eventually less able to control its own destiny, the decline is likely to be so slow in coming that it would be difficult to formulate a decisive program to head it off. That is just the point. Australia's long-term growth record for per capita income, as shown in Figure 3.1, can be interpreted either as "good enough", or as a warning that the country's standing in relation to others has begun to slip markedly in recent years. Either interpretation would be reasonable; the facts do not speak for themselves. The ten to twenty year period is more metaphorical than literal; the further one guesses into the future, the more uncertain the estimate becomes. A reformed protectionist or economically dynamic future, or a mixture of these, seems likely to give Australia a greater sense of security vis-a-vis its Asian neighbours than a business-as-usual or a premature post-industrial future.

The consequences of the choices that are made now or in the near future will not only affect the long-term future — beyond the year 2000 — but also the intervening period. Such long-term choices cast a shadow in front as well as behind. Other countries will look at the choices Australia makes in the near future and begin to judge the country on that basis, long before the full implications of these choices have reached their conclusion. Already there is a tendency in other Asia-Pacific countries to use Australia's strike record as an index of its overall performance. Because of the many (though in some ways superficial) similarities between Australia and Britain, there is a tendency to assume that the future prospects of both countries are comparable. Here, too, figures do not tell the whole story. Extrapolations from the federal government's recent study of relations with developing countries suggest that, except for Japan, which already has a higher GNP per capita than Australia (in current dollars), and possibly Singapore, the other countries of East and Southeast Asia will still have a much lower level of GNP per capita than Australia until well after the year 2000.[1] Yet the sense of direction suggested even by these conservative estimates is strong enough to affect the attitudes that Asian countries will take toward Australia between now and the end of the century. Even if various negative images of Australia's future cannot be justified by any detailed investigation, they may still be strong enough to act as self-fulfilling, or self-defeating, prophecies.[2] The issue is whether contemporary Australians want to risk bequeathing such negative images to future generations. To take an extreme example, do they want Asians to look upon Australia in roughly the same manner that Australians have traditionally looked upon Papua New Guinea or the South Pacific mini-states?

Concern for Australia's security vis-à-vis its Asian neighbours is largely long-term, and therefore relatively abstract. But if Japan, China, and the other countries of East and Southeast Asia continue to maintain higher-than-average growth rates for the rest of this century, this concern will become increasingly relevant to Australia's medium and short-term prospects.

The West and Asia

The international environment in which Australia finds itself differs greatly from that of forty, thirty, or even ten years ago. This environment is likely to change still further during the ensuing twenty years. Australia's ties to Britain and Europe, while still useful and important, are clearly less so in political terms. Australia's ties to the U.S. are also a less decisive factor than they were fifteen to thirty years ago. Western countries as a group appear weaker, vis-à-vis communist and non-Western countries, than ten years ago, although appearances can be deceptive, since internal differences among the communist and non-Western countries respectively make any such comparisons extremely crude.

No group of countries — Western, non-Western, or communist — is monolithic. Many factors can influence relationships between Western and non-Western, or communist and non-communist, countries, just as relations among various Western countries have always been complex. The non-Western countries have themselves changed in the process of modernization. The economic growth that Japan has achieved over the past century, and particularly since the end of World War II, has created almost as many similarities between contemporary Japan and Western societies as there were differences before. Correspondingly, many more differences now exist between Japan and contemporary China. Even though China, Japan, and the U.S. seem at the moment to share a strong political interest in containing the growth of Soviet power, this does not mean that important differences between China and Japan, Japan and the U.S., and the U.S. and China do not remain: China is still a communist country and a nuclear power; Japan is non-communist and a nonnuclear power; the U.S. is non-communist and a nuclear super-power.

Even within the West, there are major differences in the outlook that various countries take toward non-Western countries. Russia, historically a Western Country that shared in the expansion of European power, sees China and the U.S. — one a Confucian country, the other Western — as its chief enemies. The former imperial powers of Western Europe have demonstrated considerably less interest than the U.S. in facilitating imports of manufactured goods from the middle-income countries of East and Southeast Asia, preferring either to restrict imports of such goods in general or to negotiate preferential trade agreements on a case-by-case basis, often favouring the middle-income countries of North and West Africa at the expense of those in East and Southeast Asia. Both Europe and the U.S. see definite value in a stronger China as a partial counterweight to the Soviet union, but the U.S. has to be much more concerned than the European countries with the prospect that China might become so strong as to threaten either U.S. security interests in the Pacific or those of its Asia-Pacific allies. Japan can feel confident about China's newly affirmed desire for modernization only if it can depend on a strong American presence in the region as a counterweight to a stronger China. There is no monolithic "yellow peril", any more than in times past there was a monolithic "white peril".

Australia's political environment is now unquestionably one in which non-Western countries — particularly the economically dynamic countries of East and Southeast Asia — will have a greater say than ever before. Given Australia's geographical position — the extraordinary contrast between its ratio of land to population and that of the nearby countries of Asia — and its racial make-up and cultural background, a shift in the underlying balance of power between Western and neo-Confucian countries (where the social structure is derived from, or heavily influenced by, a predominantly Confucian cultural tradition) is bound to be more important to Australia than to most other Western countries. The economic growth of various neo-Confucian countries will not lead to a monolithic Asia. But Asia will doubtless appear more imposing to Australia than, say, to the U.S., Canada, or Britian.

The greater role that the neo-Confucian countries play in the world economy is already beginning to change long held, basically Western concepts of international relations. In traditional China, international relations were perceived quite differently from the concept that developed in Europe during the seventeenth and eighteenth centuries. This European concept was then transmitted to other parts of the world as the various European countries laid claim to territory in other continents. Before the days of European expansion, China considered itself the "Middle Kingdom" — the centre of the universe — and in those days it certainly played that role in its dealings with nearby lands over which it exerted influence. China expected these lands to pay tribute to it, both morally and financially, and by and large they did, lining up in a vertical hierarchy subordinate to China at the centre.

By contrast, the countries of post-Renaissance Europe subscribed to a concept of sovereignty, in which separate territories were entitled to at least nominal equality in their dealings with one another. In principle, each country governed its own territory, and each had a relationship to the others built on horizontal, rather than vertical, ties. With the expansion of European power over most of the world, this concept of sovereign equality became the basis for international law — and it remains so today, buttressed by diplomatic custom and enshrined in the charter of the United Nations. An altogether different system of international relations would have developed if Chinese, rather than Europeans, had set the standards for a worldwide community of nations; such a system would doubtless have been based on traditional Chinese concepts of a vertical hierarchy. Countries would be less equal in terms of a concept of sovereignty — however imperfectly applied — and more obviously unequal according to their rank in a hierarchy based on power, prestige, or both.

As non-Western countries gradually become wealthier — and the neo-Confucian countries of East and Southeast Asia are likely to be the first such group to become roughly as wealthy as the West — they will almost certainly begin to promote their own

concepts of law, equity and justice, and to think that these
deserve greater weight than they have received from Western
countries in the past. With regard to international relations, some
synthesis of Western and non-Western concepts seems likely
eventually, perhaps including not only neo-Confucian but also
Islamic or other ideas.

Japanese at times literally view international relations in two
almost mutually exclusive ways — one dominated by Western
concepts of sovereignty and the other by some as yet unformed
successor to this earlier pattern that would have a more explicitly
Japanese quality to it, emphasizing a vertical hierarchy between countries. Japanese social structure, and consequently many de facto Japanese attitudes toward other countries,
based on traditional Chinese concepts of a vertical
hierarchy. However, Japan's de jure relationship with other countries — including that with China — is clearly based on European
concepts of sovereign equality. If Japanese have a problem in this
respect, it stems from their extraordinary ability to operate in
both worlds at the same time, rather than from confusion as to
which world they are in at any one moment. Almost nothing is
more exasperating to an American or Australian businessman
who deals with Japanese companies than to see how easily they
can be sticklers for Anglo-Saxon style contractual obligations
when the provisions of a contract favour their short-term
interests, but how easily those same Japanese, if the provisions of
a contract go against their short-term interests, can relegate those
obligations to the status of a "mere piece of paper" that ought to
have no bearing on the supposed long-term mutual interests of
the two parties.

Japanese practices challenge the previously unfettered dominance of international trade by companies from predominantly
Western countries, and the particular concepts of reciprocity by
which international trade has been conducted in the past. The
inability of Western businessmen and government officials to
operate in such seemingly self-contradictory modes has been a
genuine barrier to their coming to grips with the challenges that
these Japanese practices pose. Increasingly, as Japan has become
more developed, Western countries from the U.S. down to New

Zealand have found it extremely difficult to negotiate trade concessions they felt were their due as a matter of right — based on
Western concepts of international relations — but which
Japanese officials were reluctant to grant. Part of the difficulty
that the Western countries face stems from their lack of a con-
ceptual framework as useful to them in their dealings with Japan
as the Japanese framework of selectively applying European concepts of international relations has been in Japan's dealings with
the West.

Far from seeing the problem in these terms, however, many
Western businessmen and government officials continue to
assume that the opportunity to trade with the West is somehow a
privilege for which the neo-Confucian countries ought to be grateful, and that the terms of commercial negotiations between the
Western and Asian parties ought still to be based on something
like the "treaty port" arrangements built up on the coast of China
in the nineteenth century. The tacit Western assumption has
been that the successful conclusion to normal commercial and
even political negotiations with Asian countries ought to be
brought to the Western participant on a silver platter. It is hard to
imagine a more self-deluding assumption. Even though various
Asian countries often go to great lengths to foster the notion that
it is an honour to do business with Westerners, this is little more
than a useful way of expressing the hope that profitable deals can
be arranged — certainly if they would be profitable to the Asian
party. If they are also profitable to the Western party, all the better, but that is something that is entirely the responsibility of the
Western party. Thus, Westerns often misinterpret graceful,
deferential behaviour by Asians and fail to see that the Asian
party, just like the Westerner, is also engaging in normal, profit-
seeking behaviour.

These experiences have come from Japan, but the twenty to
twenty-five year growth record of South Korea, Taiwan, Hong
Kong, and Singapore, and the growth record that China established even while hampered by the unrest of the Cultural Revolution, strongly suggest that the Japanese experience will not be
unique, and that many similar experiences are in store for
Western countries in the future. This is not to say that the neo-
Confucian countries are invincible. They, like other countries,

have strengths and weaknesses; they, too, encounter good and bad periods. But the accomplishments of the various neo-Confucian countries since the Meiji Restoration suggest that the long-term relationships that eventually develop between Western and neo-Confucian countries will be considerably affected by the choices that the predominantly Western countries make during the next twenty years.

If Western countries view the challenges posed by neo-Confucian countries with alarm, or mistakenly view these challenges as monolithic, and as a result turn inward, the world would not only be less prosperous but also more prone to political or even military conflicts along racial lines. If the West sees the drive and ambition of the neo-Confucian countries as an opportunity as well as a threat — and the differences that exist among the neo-Confucian countries as opportunities to be exploited (in the best sense of the term) — then the prospects for a continuing period of increasing prosperity throughout the Asia-Pacific region will be much stronger. The growth of the neo-Confucian countries implies that future concepts of international relations will be based on more of a synthesis of Western and neo-Confucian ideas than has been the case so far. The kind of synthesis that eventually emerges will depend at least as much on efforts made by the predominantly Western countries as on those made by the neo-Confucian countries.

Australia, because of its small population, can only play a limited role in determining which direction the West will take in these matters. But it can play some role, and whatever choice it makes will certainly have a decisive impact on its own future relationships with the nearby, far more populous countries of Asia.

Long-Term Security Policies

The most effective step that Australia could take to improve its long-term security prospects in relation to its Asian neighbours would be simply to run its economy more efficiently. Such a step — basically to a reformed protectionist or an economically dynamic future — would have a far more positive effect on the growth-oriented countries of East and Southeast Asia than further attempts to design supposedly new approaches to foreign policy. Actions here would speak much louder than words.

Japan's main interest — indeed almost its only interest — is in Australia's reliability as a supplier of raw materials. On this matter, Japanese views have already gone through a full cycle. At the moment, confidence in Australia is considerably improved, relative to the period of "resource nationalism" that reached a peak during the Whitlam government, particularly during the tenure of the late R.F.X. Connor as Minister for Minerals and Energy. Still, this recent improvement is only a relative shift, reflecting more the increased cost or unreliability of competing sources of supply than any absolute increase in Japanese confidence in Australia. The oil price increases of 1979 (the first in real terms since 1973) made transportation costs for Australian coal and iron ore much cheaper than from competing sources in the U.S. or Brazil. In the wake of the Iranian revolution, Japanese fears of an oil supply cut-off have triggered much greater efforts to switch to non-oil and/or non-OPEC sources of energy. In this context, Australia's shift away from resource nationalism since 1975 has proved extremely fortuitous. The potential Japanese demand for energy resources is so great that Australia's resource sector is almost certain to enjoy at least a mini-boom, but the chances of this are obviously increased if Japanese buyers have confidence in Australia's reliability as a supplier.

Both Japan and Australia have become "older and wiser", in their relations with each other, than they were during the mining boom of the 1960s. Though Australians have been astonished at how Japanese have sought to change provisions in a long-term contract that Australian parties regarded as fixed, Japanese have been similarly astonished at how Australians have sought to treat work stoppages as a *force majeure,* allegedly beyond their control and thus beyond the scope of contractual obligations. Where Australians have tended to regard industrial disputes as "a price that must be paid to do business in a free country", Japanese have felt justified in describing changed market conditions as a phenomenon beyond their control, and thus as grounds for renegotiating contracts.

Even though Japanese are currently increasing their dependence on Australian energy resources, they have also moved toward an unspoken policy of limiting the percentage of imports of any one commodity from Australia, to, say, 50 per cent — or to whatever level would not impair their bargaining strength. In fact, prospective increases in imports of Australian energy resources are part of a Japanese attempt to diversify energy supplies away from oil and OPEC. It would be hard to imagine that Japanese would allow themselves to become as dependent on Australian supplies of non-oil energy resources during the next twenty years as they have been for the past twenty on Middle Eastern oil.

Both Japan and Australia would like to hedge their bets — Japanese by limiting their purchases from Australia, and Australians by spreading their sales to other fast-developing countries in Asia, notably South Korea, Taiwan, and now mainland China. Yet these countries will almost certainly judge Australia's reliability as a supplier in much the same way as Japanese. Hence diversification is no justification for inefficiency — rather it should be seen as contributing to greater efficiency.

The best way to create a reputation for reliability is to be reliable. In Australia's case, this means not only operating the economy more efficiently, but also showing itself to be a responsible steward over its vast endowment of natural resources. Nearby Asian countries might easily resent the Australian's good luck in living on such rich land with so few people among whom to share the wealth. If Australians show other countries that they are in fact managing their endowment responsibly, then there is much less chance that some indignant, harder-working Asians would come to regard them as pushovers, or that the country might become a tempting target for some ambitious power that would justify an invasion on the grounds that Australians no longer deserve their continent.

In military terms, Australia's long-term security would be best assured if the U.S. were to remain the strongest single power in the world. No other balance of power in the Asia-Pacific region would be as beneficial to Australia, quite apart from whether such an arrangement would be more or less beneficial to the U.S. The relative prosperity that the Asia-Pacific countries have experienced in the last thirty-five years stems partly from the political stability provided by an American security umbrella. Even when American policies either failed to prevent war, as in Korea, or failed to achieve their main objective, as in South Vietnam, American policy was still effective enough to enable most countries in the region to benefit from being associated with the U.S.

To see how successful American policy in the Asia-Pacific region has been, one need only imagine what the region would be like today without so active an American commitment to the political independence and economic development of the non-communist countries. The Soviet Union would doubtless be the dominant power in the region, or locked in a struggle with China that, unlike the Sino-Soviet rivalry of the past two decades, would surely have spilled over into numerous conflicts-by-proxy of the sort now going on in Kampuchea. Japan would not only be much less developed, but one way or another "Finlandized" by either the Soviets or the Chinese — or else rearmed. South Korea and Taiwan would doubtless be communist. Even assuming they were not, they would probably have barely begun to develop, and the path-breaking achievements that both countries have made to world economic development would not yet have occurred. The ASEAN countries would be similarly stagnant, and either "Finlandized" or communist. Australia would be much less prosperous than it is today, if only because Japanese purchases of Australian resources would be much smaller — or perhaps nonexistent. The U.S. would also be much less prosperous, since an increasing degree of its growth can be attributed to the stimulus from the fast growing countries of Asia. More importantly, the U.S. would also be far more isolationist than it is today — or spoiling for a fight in reaction to having "lost too much" as a result of an earlier withdrawal from world affairs.

The collapse of U.S.-supported governments in Indochina unquestionably represents a failure of U.S. policy (though not necessarily of Australian policy). Nevertheless, this failure is far outweighed by the successes of U.S. policy. These certainly contributed to a change in Chinese thinking, such that Mao Tse-tung and his successors came to recognize the advantages of a strong American military and political presence in the Asia-Pacific

region. Even the Soviet Union has never really pushed for an
American withdrawal from Japan or for Japanese repudiation of
the U.S. nuclear umbrella, though its tacit acceptance of American hegemony in the region is probably more conditional now
than in years past. A strong American presence in the Asia-
Pacific region helped to create a context in which historically
unprecedented growth rates were made possible. Nothing suggests that a continued strong American presence would damage
the region's future prospects.

Any perception by the Soviet Union, China, or Japan that the
U.S. were no longer able to exercise a dominant influence in the
region would almost certainly be a prelude to the very struggles
that a strong U.S. presence has so far prevented. The Soviet
Union is already seeking to increase the range of its military
power in the region with the establishment of air and naval bases
in Vietnam. Even assuming a situation in which both the U.S.
and the Soviet Union were indifferent to the region, China and
Japan would be left vying for dominance. Both would then almost
certainly seek a position of relative strength, as much to protect
their security vis-à-vis each other as for any absolute gain. Each
would have a strong incentive to gain influence or control over
other countries in the region, such as Australia, if only to
preempt the other side. A decline of American power in the
region would lead to an intensified arms race, up to and including
the proliferation of nuclear weapons to South Korea and Taiwan,
and, as a result, to Japan, and probably also to Australia and
Indonesia.

The question of whether the U.S. will remain the strongest
single power in the world — and thus also whether the Asia-
Pacific region will continue to enjoy the benefits that American
strength has provided for the region in past years — will be
answered largely by actions that the U.S. itself takes. Australians
can, however, influence American action to some degree,
perhaps more than they realize. Typical discussions in Australia
of a U.S. role in the Asia-Pacific region tend either to take the
benefits of American protection for granted or to emphasize only
the failures. Worse yet, many discussions do not even deal with
the merits or demerits of a U.S. role in the region. Rather, they

attempt to define Australian foreign policy almost as if it could not exist unless it were to differ significantly from U.S. policy. Australia would be far more secure if the U.S. remained the dominant power in the Asia-Pacific region than under any other conceivable circumstances.

To the extent that Australia increases its ties with Asia, it would do well to increase its ties with the U.S. at the same time — and with Britain and other European countries also. An Australia that expands its ties with the U.S. and Europe would feel more secure expanding its ties to Asia. An Australia that found its ties to other Western countries weakening, or worse, that took these ties for granted, would find that all its other economic and political ties were becoming increasingly, if perhaps unwittingly, subordinate to its ties with Japan. This might place too much pressure on an otherwise fruitful, if limited, relationship.

After the Vietnam War, many Australians — and Americans — assumed there would be a permanent reduction in U.S. interest in the Asia-Pacific region. Surprisingly, perhaps, this has not happened. In fact, in certain ways, U.S. forces stationed in the Western Pacific have been greatly strengthened since 1975, although such political moves as the proposed withdrawal of U.S. ground troops from South Korea weakened somewhat the confidence that various Asian countries had in the U.S. Difficult as the U.S. position may appear to be at the moment, a recovery of American military and political power is not only a distinct possibility, but also the most effective method of assuring Australia's long-term security.

In this light, Australians might well consider ways to encourage the U.S. to retain a strong military and political presence in the Asia-Pacific region. In the wake of the Soviet invasion of Afghanistan and a consequently increased Soviet threat to the Indian Ocean (and thus to Australia's lifeline to Europe), the ANZUS treaty could well serve as a vehicle for strengthening American military and political power in the Indian Ocean area, and consequently also in the Asia-Pacific region. Far from being a historical relic — once useful as a means of securing Australian and New Zealand acquiescence to the postwar Japanese peace treaty — the ANZUS pact could be regarded as even more important for Australia's future security than it was for the past. A jointly utilized Australian-American naval base at Cockburn Sound, on the west coast of Australia, would help offset Soviet naval threats to both the Indian Ocean and Western Pacific areas. Such a base would probably also increase American awareness of Australia and Australia's security needs, as well as its own.

Attempts to promote a neutral Australia — perhaps because the presence of American bases in Australia was thought to be only a dangerous lightning rod attracting Soviet missiles, or because the effectiveness of such bases against threats from the Soviet Union or any other country was underestimated — would lead to an Australia that was either much more vulnerable to threats or much more dependent on Japan. Neither of these alternatives would seem as desirable to a majority of Australians as the present system of alliance with the U.S. A neutralist approach would very likely lead to a fearful, inward-looking backlash that would also be a less effective approach to Australia's long-term security needs than the combination of an effectively run economy and a strong alliance with the U.S.

Thus, discussions of an increased Soviet threat to the Indian Ocean are not simply a cynical replay of old anti-communist themes designed to improve the position of the Liberal party in Australian domestic politics. Whatever element of this may be in the equation, there is also an all-too-evident increase in the relative power of the Soviet Union vis-à-vis the U.S., and consequently also an all-too-evident need for the U.S. to recover its unquestioned lead, preferably in cooperation with its allies. Both the U.S. and Australia would do better to be so strong that they deter potential security threats rather than have to deal with them after they have arisen. Both would do better by acting in concert than either would by acting separately.

Will She Be Right?

Differences in Australia's rate of economic growth may well be inconsequential in the short-term and still make a very big difference in the long-term. This difference would also be felt along the way from the short to the long-term, and it would be felt even if Australia were not becoming a "treasure house" of natural resources. But the increased availability and desirability of so much natural wealth makes it all the more important for Australians to be conscious of their relationships with other countries, and particularly to be conscious of other countries' views of their stewardship over these natural resources.

No country can pick its future, at least not completely. The past is always a legacy, and the future is always unpredictable. But choices along the way do make a difference. If Australians do more now, they will have many more choices available later on; doing less will mean many fewer choices. The exact mixture between how much emphasis to put on the longer term versus the shorter term is obviously something that cannot be determined in the abstract, and that depends mainly on how Australians themselves choose to emphasize the short or the long-term.

This book provides a framework within which such choices can be made, and clarifies the pros and cons of certain alternative futures — both the likely and the unlikely. If the rest of the world were relatively static, it would be much easier to justify either a business-as-usual or a premature post-industrial future for Australia. To the extent that the rest of the world is changing — and particularly to the extent that nearby countries in Asia are changing faster than any other — a reformed protectionist or economically dynamic future is much more justified. The dynamism of Asia is more than a constraint that calls for a higher, rather than lower, growth rate for Australia. In Australia's case, unlike the U.S., Canada, or the countries of Western Europe, this dynamism is so evident it can well serve as a spur to higher growth rates.

In the past Australia's relative isolation helped shield it from many changes going on elsewhere in the world, both tangible and intangible. This same isolation will probably continue to have some sheltering influence. But if things have gone "right" in the past, they will go "right" in the future largely because Australians take steps to make them do so.

Notes

1. Report of *The Committee on Australia's Relations With the Third World* (Canberra: AGPS, 1979), pp. 92 and 212.
2. Some Japanese and Korean friends went so far as to express bewilderment as to why Hudson Institute would want to study a country they took to be as uninteresting and, except for its resources, as unimportant as Australia.

Select Bibliography

Ad Hoc Working Committee on Australia-Japan Relations, *Report* (Canberra: Australian Government Publishing Service, 1978).

Bank of New South Wales, *Review*, various issues (Sydney: Bank of New South Wales).

Donald W. Barnett, *Minerals and Energy in Australia* (Stanmore: Cassell Australia Limited, 1979).

Susan Bambrick, *Australian Minerals and Energy Policy* (Canberra: Australian National University Press, 1979).

Geoffrey Blainey, *The Rush that Never Ended* (Melbourne: Melbourne University Press, 1963).

―――――――, *The Tyranny of Distance* (Melbourne: Sun Books, 1966).

Bureau of Mineral Resources, Geology and Geophysics, *Australian Mineral Industry Annual Review 1976* (Canberra: Australian Government Publishing Service, 1978).

Bureau of Industry Economics, *Industrialisation in Asia – Some Implications for Australian Industry* (Canberra: Australian Government Publishing Service, 1978).

Manning Clark, *A History of Australia*, Vols i-iv (Melbourne: Melbourne University Press, 1962, 1968, 1973, 1978).

―――――――, *A Short History of Australia* (Sydney: Tudor Distributors, 1963).

John Crawford and Saburo Okita, *Australia, Japan and the Western Pacific Economic Relations* (Canberra: Australian Government Publishing Service, 1976).

―――――――, *Australia and Japan: Issues in the Economic Relationship* (Acton: Australia-Japan Economic Relations Research Project, 1979).

Ronald Conway, *The Great Australian Stupor* (Melbourne: Sun Books, 1971).

———————, *Land of the Long Weekend* (Melbourne: Sun Books, 1978).

Committee on Australia's Relations with the Third World, *Australia and the Third World* (Canberra: Australian Government Publishing Service, 1979).

Committee to Advise on Policies for Manufacturing Industry, R.G. Jackson, et. al, *Policies for Development of Manufacturing Industry* (Canberra: Australian Government Publishing Service, 1975).

L.F. Crisp, *Australian National Government* (Melbourne: F.W. Cheshire Pty Ltd, 1965).

Manning Clark, *A Discovery of Australia* (Sydney: Australian Broadcasting Commission, 1976).

Blanche d'Alpuget, *Mediator* (Melbourne: Melbourne University Press, 1977).

A.F. Davies, S. Encel, M.J. Berry, (eds) *Australian Society*, (Melbourne: Cheshire Publishing, 1977).

Department of Foreign Affairs, *Statements of Foreign Policy* (Canberra: Australian Government Publishing Service, 1977).

Peter Drysdale and Kiyoshi Kojima, (eds), *Australia-Japan Economic Relations in the International Context: Recent Experience and the Prospects Ahead* (Acton: Australian-Japan Economic Relations Research Project, 1978).

Flexibility, Economic Change and Growth, Treasury Paper No. 3 (Canberra: Australian Government Publishing Service, 1978).

Sol Encel, Donald Horne and Elaine Thompson, (eds), *Change the Rules* (Ringwood, Vic.: Penguin Books Australia Ltd, 1977).

Gordon Greenwood, *Approaches to Asia* (Sydney: McGraw-Hill Book Company Australia Pty Ltd, 1974).

Louis Hartz, *The Founding of New Societies* (New York: Harcourt, Brace and World, 1964).

R.J.L. Hawke, *The Resolution of Conflict* (Sydney: Australian Broadcasting Commission, 1980).

Peter Hastings and Andrew Farran (eds), *Australia's Resources Future* (Melbourne: Thomas Nelson Australia Pty Limited, 1978).

Donald Horne, *The Lucky Country* (Ringwood, Vic.: Penguin Books Australia Ltd, 1964).

———————, *Death of the Lucky Country* (Ringwood, Vic.: Penguin Books Australia Ltd, 1976).

——————, *Money Made Us* (Ringwood, Vic.: Penguin Books Australia Ltd, 1976).

Industries Assistance Commission, *Some Issues in Structural Adjustment* (Canberra: Australian Government Publishing Service, 1977).

Industries Assistance Commission, *Structural Change and Economic Interdependence* (Canberra: Australian Government Publishing Service, 1977).

Industries Assistance Commission, *Annual Report 1976-77* (Canberra: Australian Government Publishing Service, 1977).

Industries Assistance Commission, *Annual Report 1977-78* (Canberra: Australian Government Publishing Service, 1978).

Industries Assistance Commission, *Structural Change in Australia* (Canberra: Australian Government Publishing Service, 1977).

Japan-Australia Business Co-operation Committees, *Japanese Papers* (Melbourne: 1979).

Japan-Australia Business Co-operation Committee, *Australian Papers* (Melbourne: 1979).

Wolfgang Kasper, *Issues in Economic Policy* (South Melbourne: The MacMillan Company of Australia Pty Ltd, 1976).

Wolfgang Kasper and Thomas G. Parry (eds), *Growth, Trade and Structural Change in an Open Australian Economy* (Kensington: Centre for Applied Economic Research, University of New South Wales, 1978).

Wolfgang Kasper et. al, *Australia at the Crossroads: Our Choices to the Year 2000* (Sydney: Harcourt Brace Jovanovich Group (Australia) Pty Ltd, 1980).

D.A. Kemp, *Society and Electoral Behaviour in Australia* (St Lucia: University of Queensland Press, 1978).

Ronald Lawson, *Brisbane in the 1890s* (St Lucia: University of Queensland Press, 1973).

Glen Lewis, *A History of the Ports of Queensland* (St Lucia: University of Queensland Press, 1973).

Ross M. Martin, *Trade Unions in Australia* (Ringwood, Vic.: Penguin Books Australia Ltd, 1975).

D.J. Mulvaney, *The Prehistory of Australia* (Ringwood, Vic.: Penguin Books, 1975).

National Population Inquiry, W.D. Borrie et al, *Population and Australia* (Canberra: Australian Government Publishing Service, 1978).

Robert O'Neill (ed), *The Defence of Australia-Fundamental New Aspects* (Canberra: Australian National University, 1977).

H.G. Oxley, *Mateship in Local Organization*, 2nd ed., (St Lucia: University of Queensland Press, 1978).

OECD, *Australia* (Paris: OECD, 1979).

J.O.N. Perkins, *Macro-economic Policy in Australia*, 2nd ed. (Melbourne: Melbourne University Press, 1975).

D.T. Rowland, *Internal Migration in Australia* (Canberra: Australian Bureau of Statistics, 1979).

Peter Robinson, *The Crisis in Australian Capitalism* (Fitzroy Vic.: VCTA Publishing Pty Ltd, 1978).

Anne Summers, *Damned Whores and God's Police* (Ringwood, Vic.: Penguin Books Australia Ltd, 1975).

Geoffrey Sawer, *The Australian Constitution* (Canberra: Australian Government Publishing Service, 1975).

——————, *Federation Under Strain* (Melbourne: Melbourne University Press, 1977).

W.A. Sinclair, *The Process of Economic Development in Australia* (Melbourne: Cheshire Publishing Pty Ltd, 1976).

Margaret Stoneman, *Australia, Economic Prospects 1979-83* (London: The Economist Intelligence Unit Ltd, 1979).

Study Group on Structural Adjustment, Crawford et. al, *Report* (Canberra: Australian Government Publishing Service, 1979).

SRI International, *The Australia Report* (Menlo Park, Calif.: SRI International, 1978).

Maximilian Walsh, *Poor Little Rich Country* (Ringwood, Vic., Penguin Books Australia Ltd, 1979).

Russel Ward, *The Australian Legend* (Melbourne: Oxford University Press, 1958).

White Paper on Manufacturing Industry (Canberra: Australian Government Publishing Service, 1977).

Index